THEY MET DANGER

ALSO BY GORDON D. SHIRREFFS

THEY MET DANGER

REAL LIFE STORIES OF MEN WHO HAVE
BEEN AWARDED THE MEDAL OF HONOR

GORDON D. SHIRREFFS

WOLFPACK
PUBLISHING
— EST 2013 —

CONTENTS

THEY MET DANGER

THE MEDAL OF HONOR

> *War is the province of danger, and therefore, courage,*
> *above all things, is the first quality of a warrior.*

GENERAL KARL VON
CLAUSEWITZ

The boy looked proudly at his father as they walked along the busy city street. It wasn't every boy who had a major general for a father, and today, his father was in dress uniform with four rows of medal ribbons on his left breast. The boy turned and as he did, so he saw an Army enlisted man coming toward them through the crowd. The enlisted man was almost within saluting distance of the general, but as yet, he hadn't seen him. Suddenly, the boy's father snapped his right hand up to the brim of his cap. The enlisted man returned the salute, smiled a little, and then was lost in the hurrying crowd.

The boy looked up at his father in astonishment.

"But he was supposed to salute *you* first, Dad! You're an officer, and he's an enlisted man!"

The general nodded. "You're right there, son. But did you happen to see the medal ribbon he wore to the right of his other ribbons?"

The boy nodded. "Sure, Dad! It was pale blue with white stars."

The general looked back in the direction the enlisted man had gone. "That was the medal ribbon for the Medal of Honor."

The boy whistled softly. "So you had to salute him because of that?"

"No, son. There is nothing in the regulations about saluting a holder of the Medal of Honor, but whenever I see such a man, he rates a snappy salute in *my* book of regulations."

"It's a tradition then, isn't it?"

"Yes. I have a book in my library about the Medal of Honor. Suppose you read it. Then you'll see why saluting a Medal of Honor man *has* become a tradition in the Army."

* * *

The Medal of Honor for bravery *above and beyond the call of duty* is the highest point in the so-called *Pyramid of Honor*, which is composed of decorations awarded to United States service personnel for heroism in times of war. Below the Medal of Honor are the Distinguished Service Cross, the Distinguished Flying Cross, the Navy Cross, the Silver Star, the Bronze Star, and finally, the Purple Heart, which is awarded for wounds received in action.

The Medal of Honor was established by an Act of Congress during the Civil War, December 21, 1861, applying at that time only to enlisted men of the Navy. In 1862, enlisted men of the Army were included, and by an Act approved March 3, 1863, its provisions were extended to include Army officers. It is presented by a high government official, usually the President, in *the name of the Congress of the United States,* and for this reason, it is often called *The Congressional Medal of Honor.*

The present-day Army and Navy Medals of Honor differ from each other. The Army medal was designed in 1904 to replace the medal which had been established during the Civil War. It is formed of a five-pointed star in the center of which is the head of Minerva, goddess of Wisdom. The star is backed by a circle of metallic green laurel leaves. Above the star is a bar upon which is inscribed the word *Valor,* and the bar is surmounted by an eagle holding in its beak a ring, which in turn is attached to the ribbon. The ribbon is of light blue with thirteen white stars upon it. The Medal of Honor is always worn suspended from the neck.

The Navy Medal of Honor is a large five-pointed star with a medallion in the center representing Minerva warding off Discord. The medal is suspended from the ribbon by an anchor. The ribbon is the same as the Army ribbon, and the Navy Medal of Honor is also suspended from the neck.

When the medal itself is not worn, it is represented by a pale blue ribbon with thirteen white stars. The medal ribbon, being the nation's highest award, is worn to the right of all other decorations and service ribbons.

In civilian dress, a small light blue rosette, sprinkled with thirteen white stars, is worn in the buttonhole.

Today, there are approximately 350 living men who hold the Medal of Honor. Since Civil War times, when twelve hundred medals were awarded, it has become increasingly difficult to win the decoration. The American Expeditionary Force in 1917-1918 earned ninety-five medals. In World War Two, 429 were awarded. Korean Conflict fighters won 128 Medals of Honor. These totals include men from all the services.

The Army Medal of Honor award requires that there be no margin of doubt whatsoever concerning acts deserving the decoration. The deed for which it is awarded must be witnessed by two persons, and the testimony must be incontestable. It must be so outstanding that it clearly classifies the doer's gallantry as being beyond the call of duty. It must involve the risk of his life in actual combat with an enemy of the nation, and it must be the type of deed which, if not performed, would not subject him to any justified criticism.

A Medal of Honor man is entitled to additional service pay of two dollars a month, but this does not apply to officers. Both officers and enlisted men who have won the decoration are entitled to a pension of ten dollars a month when they reach the age of sixty-five. If they apply for Civil Service employment, their names are automatically placed at the top of the list. No Medal of Honor may be awarded to a man whose entire service after the time he distinguished himself was not honorable.

The present law, saying that no more than one Medal of Honor may be issued to one person, was passed in 1918. Before that time, nine men had won two Medals of Honor. Five were Army men, three were Marines, and one was a Navy man.

In this book we shall tell the stories of some of the heroic men who have been awarded the Medal of Honor from Civil War times up to and including the recent Korean Conflict. With 3,174 Medals of Honor awarded since 1862, it was a difficult task to choose the examples in the following chapters, but an effort was made to show the variety of deeds by which men have won the nation's highest award for valor on land, on sea, or in the air.

There is one certainty: *Whenever you see a man wearing the Medal of Honor, its ribbon, or its rosette, you will know you are looking at one of the "bravest of the brave."*

ONE
TWO THINGS TO SUCCEED
MITCHEL'S RAIDERS

COLD RAIN WAS FALLING STEADILY AS MORE than a score of men in civilian clothing gathered close to each other in the dark woods just off the Wartrace Road a mile or so outside of Shelbyville, Tennessee. A tall, bearded man was waiting for them. He began to speak in a quiet, confident voice, broken into now and then by the rushing of the rain-laden wind through the swaying trees or by the distant rolling thunder that wet night of April 1862.

The men knew little about the speaker other than that his name was James J. Andrews, that he was a native of Flemingsburg, Kentucky, and that he had called for a detail of thirty volunteers from the veteran Second, Twenty-First, and Thirty-Third Ohio Volunteer Infantry Regiments of Sill's Brigade for a hazardous mission.

Andrews told them the mission would take them into Confederate country in civilian clothing, which meant that any of them who were captured would quite likely be hanged as spies. He paused to give the silent men an opportunity to withdraw. None of the Ohioans moved.

Andrews continued with his talk. The volunteers had the task of paralyzing rebel communications and transportation in order to help the advance of Major General Ormsby M. Mitchel. In small groups, they would proceed to Marietta, Georgia, in the very heart of the Confederacy, to arrive on Thursday, four days from that time. The following morning, they would board the northbound mail train on its run from Atlanta to Chattanooga, capture it, and then run it to Bridgeport, Alabama, burning bridges and damaging track behind them for one hundred and thirty miles. Federal troops would be met at Bridgeport on their advance southward.

The raiders were to say they were Kentuckians on the way to join the Confederate forces if they were questioned. They had all been picked for their intelligence and daring. All of them were armed with pistols. Andrews distributed seven hundred dollars worth of Confederate money among his men, shook their hands, and then watched them depart in small groups from the dripping woods.

The next meeting of the raiders was held in Andrews's room in a Marietta hotel. Two of the volunteers had vanished and were never heard from. The weather was foul. Rain had been falling steadily throughout most of the area, which would delay General Mitchel's advance, and therefore, Andrews had decided to delay the party one day rather than run the risk of getting to Bridgeport ahead of Mitchel.

Sergeant Major Marion Ross, a senior ranking member of the party next to Andrews and a soldier of proven courage, began to feel uneasy. He suggested that the mission be abandoned or delayed, but Andrews would have none of it. When the time came, Andrews put on his high silk hat, glanced at his watch, and then crossed the muddy street to the railroad station a short time before the mail train was due.

The raiders bought tickets for various places along the line and scattered throughout the cars. James J. Andrews showed no emotion on his bearded face as he looked through the rain-wet window beside his seat. He knew that railway line like the lines on the palms of his hands, for he had traveled in this country as a trader in quinine. Actually, he was a *civilian scout* attached to General Buell's Army of the Cumberland.

The train rocked steadily northward through the rain. The raid wouldn't be easy, Andrews knew. The raiders would have to seize the train in a guarded camp, then run it for more than a hundred miles through enemy territory, overpowering or deceiving all train crews they met. Quite a task for about a score of men armed only with revolvers. They needed two things to succeed. Luck and courage. They had courage. Time would tell about the other.

* * *

The train pulled into Big Shanty Station. The tents of four Georgia regiments stood close by.

"Big Shanty Station! Twenty minutes for breakfast!" called out Conductor William A. Fuller as he walked through the cars.

Most of the passengers started for the station. Andrews beckoned to William Knight, the volunteer who was to be engineer. They strolled through the rain toward the locomotive.

The locomotive was a good one called the *General*. It was rated as one of the fastest wood burners on the Western and Atlantic. The cab was empty. There were three empty freight cars behind the tender. A sentry leaned on his rifle, watching the two men.

"Uncouple here, Bill," said Andrews calmly, pointing out the last of the freight cars.

Andrews walked through the passenger cars. "Come on, boys," he said. "It's time to go."

Knight was joined by Wilson W. Brown, the relief engineer, and George D. Wilson, the fireman. The rest of the raiders opened the boxcar doors and scrambled into the cars. Andrews nodded to Knight. The engineer pulled back on the throttle. The wheels skidded on the wet tracks and then took hold. Andrews swung up into the cab, then tipped his hat to the gaping yokel who stood guard not twenty feet away.

They had hardly gained a little speed when they heard men yelling back at the station. Step One had been accomplished. They had the train, but now the enemy knew something was up. Less than a mile from the station, the *General* began to lose speed, then slowly ground to a halt as four grim-faced men eyed each other. While the three railroad men looked for the trouble, Andrews sent little John Scott, the smallest and most agile of the raiders, up a telegraph pole to cut the wires.

The sweating men in the cab found the trouble. The draft had been shut off, and the fire was nearly out. Oil and waste soon had the fire roaring again, and the *General* took off, laying down a thick plume of smoke.

Andrews looked back across the heaving tender top. Pursuit would take time, for the nearest engines for such a purpose were either at Atlanta to the south or at Kingston to the north, each place about thirty miles from Big Shanty. He ran through the files of his excellent memory. There would be three southbound trains from Chattanooga. If the captured train was kept on its regular schedule until it reached Kingston, it would meet a local freight, the first of the three southbound trains to be dealt with by the raiders. There were eleven bridges beyond Kingston to be burned, and the telegraph and railway lines would be cut again and again.

The *General* could skirt Chattanooga by means of the railway Y below the town, then speed on into Alabama to meet Mitchel's forces. All they needed now was a little luck. *A little luck...*

Andrews kept his men busy. Now and then, the *General* came to a halt. Men piled from the cars and snatched up tools and timbers from startled road gangs held at pistol point. Rails were pried up while grinning Johnny Scott fled up the nearest splintery pole to cut telegraph wires.

The schedule of the fast mail from Atlanta was sixteen miles an hour, a laughable rate of speed in modern times, but the right of way was crooked, the roadbed was soft from the constant rains, and the rails were badly worn.

Bill Knight thrust his head farther out into the rain as they roared along. "Locomotive on a siding," he said back over his shoulder.

"Private line to the Etowah Iron Works," said Andrews.

Knight eased the throttle. "Better wreck that engine."

Andrews shook his head. "No time."

Knight eyed the ancient locomotive as they drew near to it. "They might chase us with it, Jim," he said.

"No time," said Andrews stubbornly.

They stared at the ancient locomotive as they chugged by. Its nameplate was emblazoned *Yonah*.

The men looked at each other uneasily. They were railroad men, but they were soldiers, too—men of direct action. Their leader was a man who depended more on subterfuge than on muscles. Well, he *should* know what he was doing. Still, they looked back through the rain and smoke. The old *Yonah* could be used in a chase.

Andrews felt their uneasiness. "We can wreck the tracks behind us to stop pursuit. Meanwhile, we have a schedule to keep. Keep her rollin', Bill."

* * *

Cassville loomed through the rain, and an unsuspecting railroad employee helped them load wood and water. He seemed more than satisfied with Andrews's explanation that this was a special powder train on its way to General Beauregard, who badly needed powder for his rifles and artillery.

Smoke was drifting from the diamond stack of the train for Rome, Georgia, as it waited in the Kingston yards for the mail supposedly on the captured train. As the *General* slowed to a halt, the stationmaster looked impatiently at Andrews as he swung down to the ground.

"Where is the Atlanta mail?" he demanded.

"Somewhere behind us, I expect," said Andrews in his soft Virginia drawl. "I have government authority to take this special powder train through to General Beauregard."

"You'll have to wait then," said the stationmaster testily. "The local freight is late."

There was nothing to do but wait. Andrews strolled nonchalantly up and down the platform. The three closed boxcars stood in the driving rain, with the Ohio boys inside of them, hands on cocked pistols, peering through cracks in the boxcars' sheathing.

A shrill whistle heralded the approach of the freight. Andrews met it and asked the conductor to pull up to let the powder train get through.

The conductor jerked his thumb at a wet red flag on the caboose. "You couldn't get through anyway, mister," he said. "They's another train comin' made up of everything on wheels. The Yankees are movin' south fast, and we got to get as much rollin' stock outta their hands as we can. Where you supposed to deliver that powder?"

"Corinth."

The conductor shook his head. "You can't get through to Corinth, mister. The Yankees are astride the line at Huntsville."

Andrews walked back to his waiting train. Time was running out. If Confederate soldiers in Kingston got suspicious and decided to investigate those closed boxcars...

Bill Knight and his two assistants greased the locomotive, checked the journal boxes on the cars, tapped wheels with wrenches to check them, and sweated blood as they played their part. Forty minutes dragged past and then a whistle flatted off through the rain. Bill

Knight got up into his cab, followed by Wilson and Brown.

"Thank God," said George Wilson quietly.

But the second freight train had a red flag on the caboose, too! It was running in two sections! Maybe the raiders' luck had run out. Andrews thought they might have to abandon the train.

The second section rattled into Kingston at last. Andrews was waved on. He swung up into the cab of the *General* and snapped open the cover of his watch. "One hour and five minutes late, boys," he said quietly.

"What about the two regular trains from the north?" asked Bill Knight.

Andrews gnawed at his lower lip. "We might be able to pass them at Adairsville, ten miles on. Open 'er up, Bill!"

The *General* surged onward, racing north through the rain, and some of the tension eased off among the raiders.

* * *

The people at Kingston station heard the frantic whistling of a northbound locomotive, and then the creaking *Yonah* appeared with Conductor William Fuller aboard.

Bill Fuller was no ordinary man. When his train was stolen, he had started after it on foot. Soon, he found a handcar, and he raced northward on it until he was pitched off when it hit one of the places where the Yankees had removed a rail. Then, he slogged along again on foot until he reached the *Yonah*. The *Yonah* came through proudly, making the sixteen miles from Etowah Siding to Kingston in thirteen minutes.

Fuller was told the story of the *powder train*, but he didn't believe it. The puffing *Yonah* couldn't get through the yards, so he commandeered the locomotive of the Rome train and took off through the rain, eleven minutes behind the raiders.

* * *

The raiders had stopped beyond Kingston to cut the wires and loosen a few rails. The rails were stubborn, and as the raiders struggled with them, they heard the distant whistling of a locomotive south of them. With all other locomotives racing south to get away from the Yankees, a northbound locomotive meant but one thing...pursuers. With a strength born of desperation, the raiders tore loose a rail and hurried on.

Adairsville loomed through the misty rain. A train, headed south, waited on a siding with steam up. The *General* glided slowly through the yards.

"Yuh can't get through!" yelled the stationmaster. "The Yankees have cut the line in Alabama!"

Andrews kept a smile from his face. "Can't be helped," he said seriously. "This is a *special*, with powder for General Beauregard. My orders are to get through any way I can."

"But..."

"But me no buts." Andrews smiled. "We're going through!" He glanced at the waiting train. "Better get that train out of here before the Yankees gobble her up!"

"But they's a southbound passenger train overdue now! You'll hit her head-on!"

"I'll proceed cautiously, sir, and send a flagman ahead at the curves." Andrews nudged Bill Knight. "Pull out," he said out of the side of his mouth.

The *General* chugged on. Andrews looked back. "You know, boys," he said quietly, "if we weren't in such a hurry to get this *powder* to Beauregard, I sure would like to go back and see what happens when that train meets the one that's chasing us."

The *General* raced on toward Calhoun. Andrews glanced at his watch. "Nine miles in seven-and-one-half minutes!" he said.

The fireman looked from the side window. "Top time," he said above the roaring of the exhaust, "but a mite too late. The passenger train is pulling out of Calhoun station!"

The two locomotives sped on toward each other. Whistles sounded, and then brakes were applied savagely. Sparks shot from the tortured rails. An angry red face was thrust from the cab window of the passenger train. "Back up!" roared the engineer. Andrews dropped from the cab steps of the *General*. "This train is a special for General Beauregard. Powder train. We have the right of way, mister."

"*I* have the right of way, *mister,* and I don't care where *you* think you're going!"

The passenger train conductor slogged up. "What's up?" he demanded sourly. "We're late now."

"Powder train for Beauregard," said Andrews. "I have the right of way over all trains, sir."

The engineer spat. He didn't have to *say* how he felt. But the engineer is not in charge of a train. The conductor is the boss. "Really shouldn't let you through," said the conductor.

"Listen! If this powder doesn't get through to Beauregard and his boys, it won't make any difference whether you're on time or not!"

The shot struck home. "Back 'er up," said the conductor to the fuming engineer.

The wind of freedom seemed to flow into the cab of the *General* along with the cold rain as the train rattled on to the north again, gaining speed and distance until it was safe again to cut rails and telegraph wires.

* * *

Conductor Bill Fuller had no intention of giving up the chase. He spotted a gap in the rails, knew that he couldn't get past it with his pursuit train, and started doggedly north on foot again, with his men behind him, slipping and sliding in the mud, soaked with the driving rain. He flagged down the approaching freight train south of Adairsville and had it backed to the station. There, he had the locomotive and tender uncoupled, and then he moved out on the main line, where he started north again with the locomotive in reverse. He was in luck. The locomotive was the speedy *Texas,* the fastest and best on the entire line.

* * *

James Andrews made a mental picture of the line ahead as he braced himself against the violent swaying and pitching of the *General.* The Oostanaula River bridge was a few miles away, an ideal structure to be burned.

The *General* came to a halt, and the raiders swarmed from the cars to rip up rails while Johnny

Scott scooted up the nearest telegraph pole like a tin monkey on a string to cut the wire. The thin whistling of a locomotive came from the south.

"It can't be!" said Sergeant Major Ross. "How could they get through?"

A muscle tightened in Andrews's jaw. "Let's go!" he snapped.

The rail was on a curve, and although it had not been torn loose, it was bent enough to slow down a locomotive. The raiders tumbled aboard their train. To the south, they could hear the triumphant screaming whistle of the *Texas*.

* * *

It was the first time Bill Fuller had seen his stolen train since it had pulled out of Big Shanty Station that morning.

The *Texas* raced on. Some of the men yelled at the engineer to slow down as they saw the bent rail, but he was a man made in the same mold as Bill Fuller. The *Texas* hit the bent rail, straightened it out easily, and then shot on after the fleeing *General*.

* * *

Andrews glanced back. "Put her in reverse, Bill," he said.

Knight stopped the locomotive and then put her into reverse. The rear car of the little train was empty. Andrews spoke to one of the raiders. He went down to the end of the second-to-the-last car and gripped the uncoupling pin. The *General* gained speed. Then the whistle shrilled. The raider pulled the pin as the *General* braked, and the car rolled south. The *General* shuddered and moved north again.

* * *

Fuller saw the rolling car. "Throw her in reverse!" he yelled at the engineer. The *Texas* halted, then moved slowly backward just ahead of the rolling car. When the car halted, the *Texas* moved up to it and pushed it on to the north. The chase was still on.

* * *

Andrews had gained a little time by the time they reached the Oostanaula. The raiders fired the last car. It wasn't easy, for the wood was soaked, but in time, it caught fire, and they left it blazing on the bridge while the *General* shot out of the north entry of the covered bridge like a jackrabbit out of its hole.

The *Texas* entered the covered bridge and pushed the burning car ahead of it to the far side.

Resaca was just ahead. The *General* had passed through the yards with the whistle cord held down. The *Texas* came into the yards, shoved the two boxcars onto a siding, and was off again after the Yankees, gaining every minute.

Andrews glanced back over the top of the last of the boxcars. He knew now he should have wrecked the *Yonah*. The *General* couldn't beat the *Texas*. The *Texas* must be destroyed.

Fire doors in both locomotives clanged open, and the good-pitch pine was heaved into the roaring flames while the thick smoke plumed back, beaten down by the stubborn rain. Sergeant Major Ross and his men broke open the rear of the last car. They dropped railroad ties and chunks of firewood on the rails, but the *Texas* contemptuously knocked them aside.

Fireman George Wilson held up a piece of pine. "That's the last of it," he said.

"Wood yard ahead," said Engineer Knight.

The *General* braked to a screeching halt. The raiders tumbled down and began to heave wood into the tender.

The *Texas* whistled shrilly.

"Throw ties on the rails!" commanded Andrews.

The *Texas* was forced to slow down as the *General* moved to the water tank. The hose gushed, and much of the water was lost over the top of the tender.

The *Texas* screamed like a bird of prey.

The *General* surged on. Dalton was the next obstacle to pass, ten miles on. It was a large town with a complicated system of switches and sidetracks. The *General* came to a bone-shaking halt for the usual rail-and wire-cutting.

Corporal Bill Pittinger, a young law student, came to Andrews. "Suppose we run the *General* around a curve, send men back to make a barricade, then wait for the rebel train. When she halts, we can ambush them."

Andrews tugged at his beard. The whistle of the *Texas* was haunting him now. "It's worth a try." He smiled faintly. "All we have to do is get through Dalton."

Railroad men in Dalton looked curiously at the puffing locomotive and the lone, battered boxcar. The *powder train* story was useless now. Andrews calmly swung down from the *General,* walked ahead to see if the switches would let them pass, and then waved the *General* on, swinging up on the steps as it passed by. They were in the clear once more.

* * *

The *Texas* clattered across the switch points into Dalton, dropped a man with a message for the telegrapher, then pulled out to the north, five minutes behind the *General.* Fuller's message was only partly transmitted to General Ledbetter, the rebel commander at Chattanooga, because Johnny Scott had cut the line north of Dalton, but enough of the message was received by Ledbetter to alert him.

* * *

The *General* was low on fuel again, with little chance of making Chattanooga. The raiders approached a tunnel some miles from Dalton. It was a perfect place for Pittinger's suggested ambush.

"This is the place!" he called out to Andrews.

Andrews gnawed at his thick black beard.

"All right?" asked Pittinger.

Andrews shook his head. "We'll fire the bridge over the Chickamauga River, Bill," he said at last.

There was no time to argue. "Set fire to that car," said Andrews.

The raiders worked hard to get a blaze going. Water leaked through holes in the car. The floor was soaked from the constant trampling of muddy boots. But somehow, a weak flame flickered up. The

General rumbled onto the covered bridge and dropped the car.

"Here comes that blasted rebel locomotive!" said Ross.

"Move on, Bill," said Andrews to the engineer.

Knight looked at Wilson. There was hardly any wood left for fuel and no oil at all. There was still pressure in the boiler, but it wouldn't last long without fuel.

The *General* puffed erratically through the Ringgold yards, slower and slower until, at last, it cleared the town. *How far was the next woodyard?* None of the raiders spoke. Each knew what the others were thinking.

* * *

The *Texas* approached the Chickamauga bridge. It had pushed one burning car from a bridge; it could do it again. The battered and burning car was dropped at Ringgold. The *Texas* gathered speed. It had plenty of fuel and water.

* * *

The *General* was barely moving along now. Andrews led the way by peeling off his coat and vest and throwing it into the firebox. The raiders followed his example. Bill Knight wrinkled his nose. "Journal's melting," he said.

Andrews looked at his soaked men, squatting atop the tender or crowded into the cab. He looked to the south. The rebel locomotive was in sight, trailing a thick scarf of smoke. He knew the whole countryside must be aroused by now.

Bill Knight turned to his leader. "We can't make the next wood yard," he said quietly.

The rain slanted down through the jack pine trees. It seemed to Andrews that he had suddenly become cold and wet, just as though he had not been cold and wet for hours. It had been a good try. They had almost made it. *Almost...*

The Ohio boys watched Andrews. They did not have to look south. They knew the *Texas* was biding its time now that its quarry had lost the race.

James Andrews raised his head. "Thanks, boys," he said. "Jump and scatter! And be quick!"

One after the other, the raiders dropped from the creeping *General* and sprinted for the shelter of the woods as guns opened up on them from the men aboard the *Texas*. Andrews dropped to the ground. "All right, Bill," he said. "Let her go!"

Knight threw the locomotive into reverse and jumped down to join Andrews. The game *General* started back toward its relentless pursuer, but it was no use. Steam pressure was gone, and the *General* came to a reluctant halt.

* * *

The *Texas* moved up and coupled on to its captive. From far to the south came the shrill whistling of a troop train that had been sent on after the *Texas*.

The troop train rolled up behind the *Texas* and disgorged gray-clad troops who scattered into the dripping woods after the fleeing raiders. Their orders were: "Take them, *dead or alive!*"

They took them alive—all of them.

James J. Andrews, William Campbell, who was a civilian volunteer, George D. Wilson, Marion A. Ross, Perry G. Shadrack, Samuel Slavens, Samuel Robertson, and John Scott were tried, found guilty, and hanged as spies. Fourteen of the remaining prisoners attacked their guards in Atlanta, and eight of them escaped to reach safety in the North. The remaining six were recaptured and remained as prisoners until March of 1863, when they were exchanged.

The six were sent for by Secretary of War Stanton, who gave each of them a hundred dollars and requested the State Agent for Ohio to have them commissioned as first lieutenants. The secretary then took six small leather cases from his desk and presented the first one to Jacob Parrott, the youngest of the group.

"None of these has yet been awarded to any soldier. I now present you with the first to be issued," he said. He gave a case to William Bensinger, Robert Buffum, Elihu Mason, Bill Pittinger, and William Reddick. When they opened the cases, they learned they had been awarded the first Medals of Honor in the history of the United States Army.

In time, most of the raiders received the Medal of Honor, although no man's citation specified any outstanding individual accomplishment. The citation simply stated: "For special services under General Mitchel."

Two of the raiders did not receive the Medal of Honor. One of them was the *man of mystery* of the group. William Campbell went to his execution firmly insisting that he was a soldier, an enlisted man of the Second Ohio Infantry. One version has it that Campbell was actually a newspaperman who went along on the raid for the story; another says that he was visiting friends in Company K, Second Ohio, and went along on the raid to replace a sick friend who had volunteered but who was unable to go. If Campbell *was* a soldier, there seems to be no record of his enlistment. Soldier or not, he was a brave man.

James J. Andrews, leader of the daring raid, did not receive the Medal of Honor either. He was listed as a *civilian scout* and, therefore, not eligible for an Army decoration.

Andrews and his executed comrades lie buried in the military cemetery at Chattanooga, Tennessee. It wasn't until sometime after Andrews's death that it was revealed he was known in the South as a confidential agent of the Confederate army. Perhaps Andrews planned and executed his daring raid to prove where his loyalty really lay. Who knows?

TWO
THE FIGHTINGEST MAN
DAN DALY

THE CHINESE NIGHT WAS HOT, with hardly a breath of fresh air to dispel some of the ancient stench that hung in the sweltering streets of Peking. Flames leaped and danced against the sky as flimsy wooden structures burned in the Chinese City on the south side of the Great Tartar Wall, which separated the city from the rest of Peking. Guns crackled steadily as Christian Chinese were slaughtered by the raging Chinese Boxers. The triumphant yelling of the Boxers, mingled with the pitiful screaming of the wounded and dying, carried to the silent, waiting men in the Legation Quarter. It was June 1900.

The garrison of the Legation Quarter was a curious one. It was composed of Americans, British, Russians, Germans, French, Austrians, Italians, and Japanese—soldiers, sailors, and Marines. Their strength was 409 officers and enlisted men. Three officers and fifty-three enlisted men were United States Marines. Beyond the brooding Tartar Wall, with its border of shifting light from the flames of the city, were thousands of bloodthirsty Boxers who were only biding their time before they rushed the Legation Quarter to wipe out the *yang kuei-tzu,* or *foreign devils.*

One of the United States Marines who gripped his rifle tightly and listened to the terrible sounds from the Chinese City was a New Yorker from Glen Cove, Long Island, by the name of Dan Daly. His pal grinned weakly at Dan in the darkness.

"And *you* were the leatherneck who wanted to go to the Philippines to see some fighting, Dan," he said.

The United States Legation was one of eleven legations occupying an area roughly about three-quarters of a mile square. The southern boundary of the area was the Tartar Wall, and the Wall, forty feet high and forty feet thick, was part of the defense sector of the United States forces. If Dan Daly had been disappointed in not going to the Philippines to do some fighting, he was sure now that he would get his share of fighting against the Boxers before long.

Many people had come to the Legation Quarter for protection. In some ways, their plight was not too bad. There was plenty of water and a good supply of food. The walls were stout, and the military men who defended them were of the best type, regulars and professionals. But in other respects, their position was well nigh hopeless. Each nationality had rifles of different makes and calibers. The Japanese troops had only one hundred rounds of cartridges per man. The best-provided unit had only three hundred rounds of cartridges per man. There were four pieces of light artillery within the walls. The American Marines had a Colt machine gun, hardly an efficient weapon, with 25,000 rounds.

The fighting started near the Austrian Legation, to the east. It was the most isolated of the legations and could hardly be held by the thirty-seven Austrians against the hordes of Chinese. The Austrian sailors fell back, fighting steadily. The Belgian and the Dutch Legations were abandoned on the first day of the siege because they lay too far out from the rest of the defenses. They were promptly burned by the Chinese.

Smoke swirled through the narrow streets of the Legation Quarter. Bullets thudded into the walls or screamed thinly off into space. The mingled odors of burning wood, burnt gunpowder, open sewers, and unwashed coolies were joined by another odor, that of fear. The handful of foreigners, military men and civilians, was a low-lying island in a sea of raging Chinese, and the closest relief for the besieged people was at Tientsin, over seventy miles away. The country between Peking and Tientsin was overrun with Boxers.

There was little time for Dan Daly to think about much else than fighting in the first days of the siege. The Chinese liked color, and they liked noise, and in those days, they went to war with the beating of drums, the blowing of brass trumpets, and constant screaming. It seemed to Dan and his comrades that no matter how many of the Boxers they shot down, there was always another one to take the fallen one's place. The sun was merciless, beating down into the quarter, which was enclosed by thick walls so that the wind could not get through. Burning buildings added to the heat of the Chinese summer, and although white casualties were small, due to the inaccurate shooting of the Boxers, the white troops suffered from heat exhaustion and sunstroke as they fought from behind the temporary barricades they had erected.

Dan Daly and his mates fought steadily. If they were frightened, no one could tell it by looking at them. For less steady men, the appearance and actions of the Boxers would have been almost enough to work defeat upon them without the aid of bullets and razor-edged weapons.

The Boxer color was red. A full-fledged Boxer tied his hair up in a red cloth, wore a flowing red girdle about his baggy white coolie clothing, and tied red ribbons about his ankles and wrists. Red was the color of his secret society, the *I-Ho Chuan,* a Chinese organization that took advantage of unrest in the year 1900 to fan an intense hatred against the White people, and the Japanese, who were exploiting China.

The banner of the *I-Ho Chuan* was emblazoned with a clenched fist, and the White people nicknamed society members *Boxers* because of it. The nickname stuck. Soon, the color red became the red of spilled blood. The blood of *foreign devils,* Christian Chinese, and anyone else who stood in the way!

The Boxers believed they were immune to the bullets of the *foreign devils.* Chinese magicians are among the greatest in the world, and they held public demonstrations in which swords and spears were supposedly thrust into the bodies of certain Boxers without wounding them. Bullets were apparently waved aside by a motion of the hand. If a Boxer was injured, it was explained that the unfortunate man had broken one of the rules of the Boxers or perhaps did not have true faith in the movement.

The fact was that most of the Boxers *did* believe

that they could not be hurt, and this fact didn't make it any easier on the greatly outnumbered defenders of the Legation Quarter.

China was a strange place to Dan Daly and his mates. Dan had enlisted in the United States Marines just as the Spanish-American War ended in 1898. He had expected to be sent to the Philippines, where there was still plenty of fighting going on. Instead, he and some of his mates were sent to China. The Marines, along with troops of other nations, were transported to Peking just in time to get into the Legation Quarter in front of masses of glowering Chinese who lined the roads.

Trouble had begun to pile up. Some Belgian railroad construction engineers had been massacred. Missionaries had been beheaded. A Japanese secretary had been murdered. The German ambassador, a brave and headstrong man, had ventured out to talk with Chinese authorities and had been shot to death by a Boxer.

The siege was soon in full swing. The Americans, with German troops, held a vital sector, part of which was a section of the looming Tartar Wall. The sector was practically under the artillery of the enemy above the main city gate. The Marines and their German comrades had to hold that wall. If the wall was captured, the Legation Quarter could not be held. The fighting was closed in and vicious, with no quarter asked or given.

The siege dragged on and on, with no sign of relief from Tientsin. The lines of defense began to shrink week by week, and fires raged day and night. The Italian, Austrian, French, Dutch, and German Legations were either burned completely or gutted for the most part. Those defenders who were captured were beheaded and their heads placed on pikes at the city gates to look down with set grins on the Legation Quarter. The defenders fought fires almost as constantly as they fought the Boxers themselves.

Dan Daly was in the thick of it. He saw men die violent deaths for the first time in his life, but the tough little fighter seemed to thrive on battle. The Boxers used nine-pounder Krupp guns to batter away at the American and Russian Legations which were side by side. Sandbags were hastily improvised from silks and satins, the legs of old trousers, and anything else that could hold earth.

On the twenty-fourth of June, the American Marines and the Germans charged along the top of the Tartar Wall and met the Chinese defenders in a vicious hand-to-hand fight on the roadway that was atop the wall. It was cut and thrust, parry and shoot, and the Chinese fell back beneath the savage onslaught. Right in the front rank, wielding bayonet against spear and sword, was Dan Daly. The Marines and Germans held the wall top until a gang of Christian Chinese, under the command of a fighting missionary, could build a barricade.

Dan Daly was one of the defenders of the barricade. The Boxers built their own defenses farther along the wall, but as long as the American-German barricade was there, and was held, it prevented the Boxers from gaining a position directly above the other defenders of the Legation.

The fighting on the Tartar Wall was almost continuous. Captain Myers of the United States Marines was wounded in a charge composed of his own men, Germans, Russian sailors, and British Marines. Two Marines died, and the captain was wounded by a spear.

July 15 was an exceptionally hot day from the standpoints of both weather and fighting. Captain N. H. Hall, who had relieved the wounded Captain Myers, decided to scout along the dangerous wall to find a better position for the defenders to erect a barricade. He took one man with him, Dan Daly.

They worked their way along the wall for a hundred yards while Mauser bullets whined past them. Soon, Captain Hall found a bastion that would serve the purpose. But the Chinese were massing in the dimness to prevent the defenders from building their barricade. Captain Hall went back along the bullet-swept wall to bring up Christian Chinese to build the new sandbag barricade at the bastion while Dan Daly stood there alone with a bayoneted rifle in his hands.

Flames lighted up the evening sky. Now and then came the dull, coughing thud of an artillery piece over the constant crackling noise of rifle firing. Dan felt the warm, itching sweat running down his sides, and his tongue was dry in his mouth with a brassy taste to it. He squinted his eyes, looking along the wall toward the Chinese barricade several hundred yards away. If the Boxers came now...

Bullets thudded into the ancient masonry of the bastion. Below the wall, to the south, was the great moat that paralleled the Tartar Wall, and the stench of floating, bloated corpses hung in the hot air with a sweet-rotten odor that penetrated a man's lungs. Dan wiped each hand in turn on his dirty shirt and peered into the dimness with eyes that stung from the salt sweat that trickled from beneath the brim of his hat. He thought longingly of Glen Cove and the breeze that blew in from Long Island Sound with a salty tang to it.

He looked back over his shoulder. Those Christian Chinese were a long time coming. A single man could get awfully lonely on that wall. He turned his head and thought he saw something moving in the darkness. He dashed the sweat from his face and crouched a little, as though to see better. There *was* something moving in the darkness.

Then, as though they had been conjured out of the thick-smelling air by a Chinese magician, he saw Boxers moving along the wall toward his bastion. There were a lot of them, too many for one man—unless that man was a United States Marine who had been told to *hold* his position. Flickering firelight from a burning building glinted from naked two-handed swords and sharp spear tips as the Chinese moved swiftly toward the bastion.

Snipers opened fire, but as usual, they fired too high. The Chinese believed that the *higher* a rear sight was raised, the *faster* the bullet went. Even so, there were plenty of slugs whistling past Dan Daly as he waited for the assault.

They started to run toward the bastion. Dan raised his rifle and opened fire, picking off the leaders, but still, the others came on.

"*Sha! Sha!*" they yelled. "Kill! Kill!"

"*Sha! Sha!*" mimicked Dan as he emptied his rifle. One cartridge for one man, that was the Marine way. But now there was no time to reload, no time to look back for help, no time for anything but the cold steel of the bayonet. The bayonet fighter kills or is killed.

A raging fury of a man, handling a heavy rifle

tipped by sixteen inches of bayonet blade, drove in on the yelling Chinese without a word. There is a cold precision to bayonet fighting, and US Marines have few peers in the use of the most ancient of all modern weapons.

A long thrust sank the blade into the chest of a screaming Boxer. Twist and withdraw. Short thrust into the side of another sword-wielding Boxer. Withdraw, parry a spear thrust with a harsh grating of metal and wood, then swing up the steel-shod rifle butt to crash it against the head of another enemy. Then slash hard, right and left, to clear a little fighting space for Dan Daly, US Marine, so that he could get his rifle butt tucked beneath his arm, set against his side for the long thrust again.

The fight took only a few minutes. Dan Daly held the wall with rifle and bayonet until reinforcements raced up to him. They added their fire to his where he stood with a heap of dead and dying Boxers at his feet, sweat dripping from his red face, his shirt black with perspiration, and the firelight glistening on the wet blade of his bayonet.

* * *

There was still a lot of fighting to be done to defend the Legation Quarter against the Chinese. It wasn't until August 14 that a mixed column of troops, the International Relief Force, ended the Siege of Peking after hard and bitter fighting by Japanese, Russian, British, American, French, German, Austrian, and Italian troops.

Dan Daly was awarded the Medal of Honor for his

heroism on the great Tartar Wall on the evening of July 15, 1900. But Dan wasn't through yet. He served for a time in Cuba and was with the United States Marines who landed at Vera Cruz, Mexico, in the face of armed Mexicans in 1914.

In October 1915, Gunnery Sergeant Dan Daly was in Haiti fighting against the Cacos, rebels who held Haiti in bloody fear. While his thirty-five-man detachment was crossing a rain-swollen river, they were taken under fire by the Cacos. None of them was hit, but one horse was killed. Although there were an estimated four hundred of the enemy in the wet brush ahead, the thirty-five Marines prepared to attack.

They crossed the river and plunged into the jungle after the Cacos. The detachment commander called for his machine gun to be set up. No one was sure where the machine gun was, but Sergeant Daly made a guess. It was strapped to the back of the dead horse back at the river crossing.

Dan Daly turned quietly back through the wet, dark jungle to get that gun.

Mauser bullets whispered past his head as he worked his way back toward the river. He reached the bank, but he couldn't find the horse. He plunged into the water and felt about for the dead animal until he found it, then cut the lashings loose and dragged the heavy gun to the bank. For nearly a mile, he crawled through the bullet-riddled jungle growth with the heavy gun on his back.

For that deed, and his courageous performances the next day against the Cacos, he received his second Medal of Honor, the only enlisted marine ever to be so honored in the fighting history of the Corps.

Dan Daly's story could have stopped the time he won his first Medal of Honor atop the bullet-swept Tartar Wall, and it could well have stopped in the wet jungle of Haiti in 1915. But with Gunnery Sergeant Daly, it just couldn't be so. He was getting old for a fighting marine in 1917 when America entered the First World War. He was forty-four and could well have been left behind in the States at a desk job or as an instructor. But anyone who knew Dan Daly knew where he would end up...in France.

Dan was at Belleau Wood in June 1918. At Lucy le Bocage, the Americans had established a field dressing station for the many wounded and, foolishly enough, an ammunition dump as well. German artillery fire set the small arms ammunition to blazing. If the conflagration spread to the stores of big artillery shells...

But somehow, there was a tough little marine sergeant around by the name of Dan Daly. He went in and put out the fire. On the morning of June 10, Dan Daly spotted an enemy machine-gun nest that had been giving his company trouble. Sergeant Daly moved in on it armed with grenades and an automatic pistol, and when the smoke cleared, he was still on his feet, and the enemy machine-gun nest did not exist. Two days later, he was wounded and shipped off to a hospital, but he made his way back into action in October of 1918.

Dan Daly was born on November 11, 1873. Exactly forty-five years later, on November 11, 1918, the Armistice ended World War One, but Dan Daly didn't do much celebrating. He had been wounded a second time in October during the Champagne Offensive.

Gunnery Sergeant Dan Daly died April 28, 1927.

Along with his two Medals of Honor, he was entitled to wear the Navy Cross, the Distinguished Service Cross, the French *Medaille Militaire,* and other decorations for his services in Belleau Wood in 1918. Dan was a *Marine of Marines.* During World War One, the Germans feared the Marines to such an extent that they nicknamed them *teufelhunden* or *devil dogs.* The name stuck to the Marines and also to Dan Daly, for he was known throughout the Corps as *Devil Dog Dan.*

Marine General Smedley Butler called Sergeant Daly, "the fightingest man I know." The general himself was highly qualified to make that statement. Nine men in the history of the Medal of Honor have been decorated twice with that most rare of all military decorations. One of them was Dan Daly. General Smedley Butler was another.

THREE
ONE-MAN ARMY
ALVIN C. YORK

SUNLIGHT CAME DOWN through the foliage in brilliant shafts through which dust motes whirled ceaselessly. It was quiet in the long clearing except for the faint gobbling of a big tom turkey. The lean, redheaded mountaineer raised his long-barreled, muzzle-loading, cap-and-ball rifle and sighted it.

A log lay at the far end of the glade, forty yards away, and above it now and then appeared the head of the tom turkey. The watching men wet their lips as a fitful breeze crept through the woods. Then the rifle cracked flatly, and the turkey's head jerked and disappeared.

Some of the men shook their heads and smiled. A bearded old hunter raised a hand. "Ain't no doubt but what Alvin York here wins the turkey shoot!" he said.

"As usual," said one of the younger men sourly.

A boy went for the turkey and brought it back to the tall mountaineer. "Plumb center, Alvin," he said proudly.

Alvin slung the turkey over his shoulder and

walked back toward the little mountain hamlet of Pall Mall. A man leaning against a tree waved a hand as he passed. "Ye figurin' on goin' to the war, Alvin?" he asked.

Alvin stopped. "I don't hold with killin' people."

"Them Germans don't feel that way."

The redhead nodded. "I can't help that. But the Church of Christ in the Christian Union don't hold with killin' folks."

"Ye might be drafted, Alvin."

Alvin straightened up. "I'm registered," he said quietly. "But I wrote on the notice that I didn't want to fight."

"Ye figure bein' what they call a conscientious objector?"

"Somethin' like that."

Alvin walked toward home. Pall Mall, Tennessee, was a back-eddy of the surge of American progress. It was on the Cumberland Plateau, in a sheltered valley named the *Three Forks of the Wolf*, where the speech was an old form of English, and the people lived in the year 1917 much as their pioneer ancestors had lived a hundred years before. They were deeply religious, and they lived their religion every day.

The Cumberland Plateau was still wilderness country, and hunting and trapping were the recreation of the men because they had been brought up that way since childhood. Most of them were skilled woodsmen and deadly shots, and their proud history in such matters was better known to the outside world than anything else about them.

Alvin York was a descendant of pure pioneer blood, one of eleven children of William York, a blacksmith, who had raised his big brood in a simple two-room board-and-batten cabin. The boy had received his sketchy smattering of the *Three Rs* and a liberal dosing of the Bible, shooting, and woodcraft. He was given his first rifle at an early age, and in time, he had become one of the top marksmen in the Saturday turkey and beef shoots.

When the news of the war with Germany finally penetrated the *Three Forks of the Wolf*, the old-timers thought at first that the United States was again at war with England, and when they learned that England was an ally, they viewed the friendship with suspicion. There were few volunteers from the mountain country.

Alvin York did not believe in war. "For all they that take the sword shall perish with the sword," was his belief. The rules of his church forbade war, and besides, he was the principal support of his mother. He had clear grounds upon which to claim exemption from the draft, but that was not Alvin York's way. He did not believe in war and killing; he *did* believe it was necessary to serve his country.

* * *

In November 1917, he reported to Camp Gordon, Georgia, and three months later, he was assigned to Company G, 328th Infantry, Eighty-Second Division, nicknamed the *All-American* Division. It had originally been composed of men from Georgia, Alabama, and Tennessee, but in time, like most of the other divisions of the American Army, it had men in it from many other states of the Union.

Alvin was doing his duty, but his conscience still

bothered him. He knew he might be ordered into battle and that he might have to kill men. His mother and his pastor had written to Alvin's superior officer to state that his religion forbade war. His officers knew that he was not a coward; he was sincere and open in his beliefs. They explained the causes of the war to him, using the Bible to prove that while peace was desirable, it should not be a peace at any price. And, though it was a hard struggle for the tall, redheaded mountaineer, he gradually began to believe that, in this case, it was God's will that he should fight.

By the time the Eighty-Second Division reached France in May of 1918, Alvin was recognized as one of the finest shots in the organization, particularly at moving targets. By the time the division entered the bloody Meuse-Argonne offensive on October 9, 1918, he had earned corporal's stripes and command of an automatic rifle team.

The men of the veteran Eighty-Second Division moved up into the line through cold rain. Three divisions had advanced into the Argonne Forest, but only one of them, the Regulars of the First Division, had managed to advance to its objective. The flanks of the First were being swept by enemy fire. The Eighty-Second Division was ordered to advance the lines on the left flank of the First Division in an attack on Chatel-Chehery Hills.

The men of the Eighty-second knew they were in for a fight. The Argonne Woods had many high places from which the Germans could pour down deadly and accurate fire. The woods were pathless, cut through by deep ravines, swamps, and ridges. Constant chilling downpours turned the shell-torn ground into thick, clinging mud.

Six companies of the 308th Infantry, one company of the 307th Infantry, and a platoon of the 306th Machine Gun Battalion of the Seventy-seventh or *Liberty* Division had been cut off for five days in the dripping tangle of woods. History knows them as the famed *Lost Battalion*. Units of the Twenty-Eighth and Eighty-Second Divisions reinforced the Seventy-Seventh Division to help them get the *Lost Battalion* out of the trap.

Shells exploded in the thick mud and threw geysers of smoke and steel over the crouching men of Company G, who clung to the battered sides of Hill 223. Rain slanted down to mingle with the smoke. Now and then, the rattling of Maxim machine guns came from the hills held by the Germans.

Corporal York lay in a foxhole, wiping the mud from his rifle. Now and then, he looked toward the German lines. There wasn't much to shoot at. Across five hundred yards of valley were three hills, the middle one rough and rugged, the other two more gentle. Those three hills were held by a tough division of veteran German troops.

An officer crawled in beside Alvin and focused his field glasses on the hills. "We've got to take those hills, York," he said quietly to the big soldier.

"Won't be easy, sir."

"No, but behind those hills is the narrow-gauge railway that brings up their supplies. That's our objective."

Alvin shifted in the cold mud. "When do we jump off, sir?"

The officer lowered the glasses and looked at the redheaded corporal. "Six o'clock in the morning, York."

The thick, chilling mist lifted a little just before the Second Battalion of the 328th was to jump off. All along the battered side of the hill, 223 men got ready for battle. Rifles had been wiped clean of mud. Bayonets had been fixed. The soldiers lay in the mud and eyed the hills across the valley.

Whistles blew, and the men moved out. York plodded on through the mud with his squad. "There's a chance," he said encouragingly. "Maybe they can't see us through the mist."

No one spoke.

Then, "There's the sun," a shivering private said.

The sun began to burn away the mist. Suddenly, machine guns stuttered along the line of hills, and a metallic sleet swept the American lines. In the distance, the whistling of shells could be heard, and seventy-seven-millimeter-high, explosive and shrapnel burst along the advancing lines. The men plunged on. Then machine-gun fire ripped into their flanks and began to drop them in heaps. The attack faltered, slowed down, and stopped completely as the men sought cover. It was too much for flesh and blood to stand.

Smoke mingled with the drifting mist, giving an unreal quality to the torn and battered landscape. The Maxims still stuttered, seeking out the attackers with savage intensity. The Second Battalion was out of business, or so it seemed.

Sergeant Harry Parsons squirmed through the mud, slipping from shattered tree trunk to water-filled shell hole until he reached Corporal York. "Our platoon has to take care of those flanking machine guns, Alvin," he said quietly.

Alvin whistled.

"Three squads," said Parsons. He shook his head. "Sixteen men left out of the original twenty-four."

"We'll do the best we can," said Alvin York.

Parsons led the understrength platoon toward the flanking machine guns. Bullets whipped through the brush, and now and then, a shell burst in the wet woods, throwing up geysers of mud and splintered wood. Then machine guns rattled from the right flank.

Sergeant Parsons eyed the deadly hills from under the brim of his helmet. "Those buzzards are watching the valley, not the slopes, Tennessee," he said. "So we go up the slopes."

Parsons led the way, belly flat on the wet ground. Then he stopped and waved York up. "Look," he said.

A winding trail was in front of them. York whistled again. "We're behind their lines, Harry," he said softly.

They could still hear the chattering of the machine guns, but the guns were behind them now.

"Look!" gasped one of the men.

Two Germans, wearing their heavy coal-scuttle helmets, had appeared, carrying a stretcher. Rifles cracked as the Americans tried to stop the Germans from revealing the platoon's hiding place. One of the Germans was wounded, but both of them escaped into the woods.

Parsons stood up. "Let's go!" he snapped. He led the way across a little stream. There was no time to waste.

Ahead of the charging Americans was a clearing, and grouped about a hut were half a hundred of the enemy. The Americans opened fire. The sudden attack was a success. The Germans thrust their arms into the air. *"Kamerad! Kamerad!"* they yelled.

The Americans moved up. "This must be their battalion headquarters," said Parsons.

York was at the far left of the American line. He turned his head and saw Germans hastily moving their machine guns to open fire on the platoon. A German cupped his hands about his mouth and yelled at the prisoners. Some of the Americans dropped to the ground at the same time the prisoners did. A scythe of machine-gun fire swept through the woods and caught the Americans who had not dropped. Sergeant Parsons and two of his men were wounded, while six others died instantly.

Alvin York dived for cover and bellied through the wet brush. "Stay under cover!" he yelled over his shoulder.

He peered through the brush. Ahead, he could see the enemy peering down toward the other Americans. Some of the Germans started down the slope. York opened fire. One German dropped. The others scuttled back to the guns and opened up again.

York wet his lips and waited. A helmeted head showed. He fired. The helmet flew off, and the man fell. Bullets keened through the brush, trying to find the hidden sharpshooter.

Smoke drifted through the woods. York moved a little now and then. When he spotted a German, he fired. The targets were bigger than a turkey's head at forty yards, but there was a major handicap in this type of marksmanship. The target could shoot back.

It grew quiet in the wet woods. The Germans were

crawling about, trying to outflank York, but his rifle bullets found them out. "Surrender!" he called and then ducked as bullets tore through the brush about him.

It was quiet again; it was *too* quiet. On the slope above, a German moved. Alvin fired and then drew back his rifle bolt to eject the last shell case.

Suddenly, he heard hoarse shouting, and a little knot of Germans charged him with fixed bayonets. His rifle was empty. He dropped it and drew out his forty-five-caliber automatic pistol. He knew instantly that if he fired at the first German, the others would seek cover, then open fire on him, and he wouldn't have a chance. And so he calmly fired at the *last man first,* then at the next man, until the first man was charging York alone. The pistol cracked for the sixth time, and the leader went down to join his fallen comrades. Without realizing it, Alvin York had started a shooting trick that has been an unofficial doctrine in the Army ever since.

He swiftly reloaded his rifle and pistol and shifted his position. The machine guns rattled angrily, trying to find this deadly marksman who was making a fool out of veteran German combat troops.

Alvin rested his rifle on a log. He sighted and fired. One machine gunner fell sideways from his chattering weapon to be replaced by another gunner who didn't have time to fire before a rifle bullet caught him between the eyes. In less time than it takes to tell, the entire crew was dead or wounded.

"*Amerikaner!*" a German officer yelled. "I surrender the battalion!"

Alvin York shifted his hot rifle. "Do it and I'll treat ye white!" he yelled back.

There was a movement in the wet brush. A German appeared, yanked the cord on a potato-masher grenade, and hurled it at York. The grenade went wide, exploded, and sowed hot, tinkling metal in the brush. The American's rifle cracked, and the grenadier died instantly.

That was the final straw for the German officer. He blew his whistle and ordered his men to surrender. All through the woods, the Germans stood up, dropped their weapons, and raised their arms. York marched them back toward his comrades who had been unable to help him in his one-man fight against great odds but had kept others of the enemy from reaching his rear.

Alvin formed his parade of prisoners two by two. Germans carried wounded Sergeant Parsons. On each flank were posted Americans with orders to shoot to kill at the first sign of treachery. Corporal Alvin York led the way with the German major in front of him and German officers on either side.

The unshaven and bone-weary redhead from Tennessee held his deadly rifle in his hands as he marched through the woods with well over a hundred veteran German troops behind him, none of them daring to make a move toward him. It was incredible—it was impossible—yet it was happening.

More and more Germans surrendered and joined the strange column. When they reached the American lines, openmouthed Yanks stared at York and his prisoners.

"You bringing in the whole German Army, York?" asked one of them.

He didn't bring in the whole German Army. Just 132 Germans, including a major and two other officers.

He had captured thirty-five machine guns, killed about twenty of the enemy, and put a veteran German machine gun battalion completely out of business. A grim record for a man who had not believed in war in the first place!

* * *

The Eighty-Second Division fought on for three more weeks. Alvin York received his sergeant's stripes, and a brigade review was held in his honor. He was personally decorated by President Poincare of France.

When he returned to the United States in May of 1919, the House of Representatives in Washington stopped debate to cheer him when he appeared in the visitors' gallery. He was offered $75,000 to appear in a motion picture about the war, a thousand dollars a week to appear in vaudeville. Anything and everything was his for the asking. He refused it all. To sell his war record would be like putting a price on patriotism, he said.

Later, Alvin decided he would put his fame to some use. He wanted to establish proper schools for the hill children, and since the people of Tennessee had been collecting an Alvin York Fund, he had them turn the money into a foundation for building schools in the mountains. All he accepted for himself was a small farm.

As this book is being written, Alvin York is bedridden in his hometown of Pall Mall, Tennessee. He still smiles at life, for nothing can beat such a man. He recalls that his feat in World War One won him the Medal of Honor and many other decorations, as well as the name of the *One-Man Army*. And perhaps he smiles to himself, thinking it is all part of a pattern. Sergeant Alvin Cullem York is a direct descendant of frontiersman Davy Crockett, who wasn't a bad hand with a rifle, *and* a war, himself.

FOUR

THE BALLOON BUSTER
FRANK LUKE

HE COULD SEE for miles in every direction. The winding trenches far below him were straggling lines on the dun earth. To his right were brilliant flashes of light where antiaircraft shells burst in cottony white puffs. He knew they were friendly guns firing, for French and American antiaircraft shell bursts were white as compared to the black puffs of the German Archies of World War One.

The powerful Hispano-Suiza engine of his stubby Spad pursuit plane hummed steadily. Ahead of him and a little to his right was the Spad flown by his commanding officer, Major Harold E. Hartney, a top veteran pilot who had flown with the British Royal Air Force and was an ace, having shot down five planes before transferring to the United States Air Corps.

Frank Luke grinned to himself. This was the real McCoy, flying in combat formation with ten other planes to protect the slow-flying, clumsy photographic planes below them. Frank kept turning his head from one side to the other. They had told him at the Third Aviation Instruction Center at Issoudun that if you didn't see a Jerry plane first, you might never get a second chance. He didn't see any Jerry Fokkers or Halberstadts, but he did notice that one after the other, Spads of the flight were dropping behind, and already some of them had returned to the flying field.

The Spads that had been issued to the Twenty-seventh Aero Squadron were almost junk, planes that had been used by the French and then turned over to their American allies. The old Spads had poorly housed reduction gears, and these caused constant trouble. When an engine began to miss, the pilots had been firmly instructed to head for home.

Black puffs of German Archies began to appear in the clear sky. The Americans were well over the enemy lines now. Frank's Spad bucked and rolled in the disturbed air, but he kept close to Hartney's plane, seeing the mustached face turn anxiously toward him now and then. It wasn't until Frank took a good look behind him that he knew why Hartney appeared so worried. Frank was the only member of the formation left other than Hartney. The others had headed for the home field at Coincy.

Frank glanced at his altimeter. Eighteen thousand feet, and it was beginning to get hazy from the heat of the day. He looked up. A plane was high above them, in the sun. Squinting his eyes, he tried to identify it. They had told him it was best to attack from the sun.

He saw the plane tip downward and plunge toward Hartney's plane. In a moment, Frank saw there were bright red-orange flashes from the strange plane's machine guns and the swift streaks of tracers lancing toward Hartney. Hartney half rolled, then dived, trusting to the solid construction of the Spad, until he was out of sight in the clouds below. The German Fokker climbed a little. Frank Luke gunned his Spad and began to creep up on the enemy plane. The plane began to spiral in descent, but Frank never let him out of his sight.

Closer and closer he flew until it seemed as though the very noise of the Spad's big engine would alert the German pilot, but he never turned his head. Frank closed his hand on his control stick, and his twin Vickers machine guns began to chatter. The tracers lanced down into the German's cockpit, and the pilot stiffened, turned his head, then went into a roaring power dive. Frank followed, rapping out bullet after bullet with his twin guns.

The ground was shooting up toward them now, but Frank Luke didn't stop. It seemed as though every round was pouring into that cockpit. Then, the ground was dangerously close. He pulled back on the stick and shot off in level flight not two hundred feet above the scarred earth. He glanced back. The Fokker had struck the ground, and a column of smoke and flame lanced up into the air.

Score one for Frank Luke, the kid from Arizona.

They were waiting for him on the field at Coincy. He could see the white faces turned up toward him as he circled the field, gunning his engine to let them know he had scored. He came in for a landing with the wind whistling through the wires, idled to a halt, and before the wheels had hardly stopped turning, he was out of the cockpit.

"I got one, Major!" he yelled. "Yippee! He was on your tail, but I got him! I never opened up until I had my guns right in that baby's cockpit! I didn't leave him until he hit the ground in flames with me not more than two hundred feet behind him!"

Hartney eyed the excited kid. The rest of the pilots grinned and walked away. "There goes the Arizona Boaster again," one of them said.

Another pilot spat, "He was blowing this morning that he'd get his first Boche today or he wouldn't come back. I *knew* he'd claim one."

Frank Luke peeled off his goggles and helmet and looked at Hartney. "Well, sir?" he said quietly.

Hartney tugged at his mustache. "I believe you, kid."

"What's the matter with them?"

Hartney shrugged. His eyes met Frank's. "You have to admit, Luke, that you've been shooting off your mouth a lot around here. Some of these boys are good pilots with a lot of over-the-lines experience. You've been rubbing them the wrong way."

The firm jaw seemed to stiffen. "That don't bother me, sir."

The wise eyes studied the boy's face. "No? Listen, kid, you're quick-tempered, cocky, too talkative, and have a bad habit of ignoring good advice. Now listen to me: Before you brag anymore, you had better *show* them what you can do, then shut up about that, too."

Frank Luke's eyes hardened. "Then you don't believe me either, sir?"

Hartney slapped the boy on the shoulder. "Certainly, I do! You might not be the best flyer in this squadron, but there isn't a pilot in it who can shoot like you can. Come on! Let's see if we can get that victory confirmed!"

But it was no use. No one had seen an enemy plane crash in the area where Luke claimed he had shot down the Fokker. It was what his squadron mates had expected.

* * *

Frank Luke lay on his bunk that night, alone in his quarters, staring up at the ceiling. He knew he had scored. The door opened, and Joe Wehner, another pilot, came in. "Hi, Frank," he said. "Congratulations!"

Frank got up on one elbow. "I got that baby, Joe," he said earnestly.

Joe Wehner was quiet and easygoing. He had had troubles of his own since joining the Air Corps and earning his wings.

In those days of World War One, there was a great deal of bitterness in the United States toward anything German, whether or not it was connected with the war. Sauerkraut became known as Liberty cabbage! More than one serviceman was persecuted because of his German ancestry and name. Joe Wehner was one of these. He had been arrested and questioned during his training days in the States and again just before embarking for England in February of 1918. These investigations hurt him deeply, and he had learned to keep pretty much to himself.

For some odd reason, the two young men got on well together. The brash and cocky Frank Luke and the quiet and easygoing Joe Wehner became fast friends. Frank was of German descent, too, but he had never been bothered by investigations. There was one thing he did know: Joe Wehner was as fine a patriot as any man in the American Expeditionary Force.

Frank Luke was born in Phoenix, Arizona, in 1897. He had been a star athlete in high school and had worked in the copper mines at Ajo during the summer. He had become a crack shot with rifle and pistol.

In September of 1917, he enlisted in the Signal Corps with the idea of becoming a fighter pilot, for in those days, aviation was considered a function of the Signal Corps. Things moved swiftly for Frank. He trained in Texas, and in San Diego, California, he received his pilot's wings in January of 1918. He had sailed for France in March.

They had kept him busy enough after his arrival in France. He had received his advanced flying training at Issoudun and instruction in aerial gunnery at Cateau. Later, he served as a ferry pilot at Orly, gaining much experience in flying various types of aircraft, but he kept pestering his commanding officer for a transfer to combat duty. On July 26, 1918, he joined the Twenty-seventh Aero Squadron of the First Pursuit Group then stationed at Saints.

Those were hectic days in the late summer of 1918. The new American Air Service was facing veteran German pilots flying fast and maneuverable Fokker, Halberstadt, and Pfalz pursuit ships. Many Europeans believed the Americans could not fight. The French, British, and Italian losses had been terrible ones. Foreign generals wanted to incorporate American units into their armies, but General John J. Pershing, commander of the AEF, refused to allow it. The Americans would fight as an *American* Army and as an *Amer-*

ican Air Service. Now the Americans, on the ground and in the air, would have to prove that he had made the right decision.

* * *

Frank was on patrol on September 12 near Marieulles. He didn't spot an enemy plane, but while banking steeply, he saw something that took his interest. It was a great, swollen-looking object swaying in the sky. It was an observation balloon used by artillery observers to spot the shooting of their guns and to correct the fire. The observers also looked for enemy movements and concentrations.

Frank banked again, eyeing the swaying hulk eagerly. The bloated thing hung at about 2,500 feet. He fired his guns to warm them up and to make sure they were in good operating order. He had never been given credit for his first victory, the Fokker he had shot down, because no one had confirmed it. This time, he was going to score a victory that would be *sure* to be seen.

He tipped the little Spad down into a dive, aiming for the balloon. The huge black Maltese cross on the side was his target. Closer and closer he came to it. Then he saw black puffs of Archie and flashing objects known as *flaming onions* streaking past him, as well as tracers. The ground about the balloon was a veritable hornet's nest.

The balloon began to move slowly downward. The bulk of the target now filled his ring sights. He opened fire. The Spad shivered from the vibration of the guns. Metal sang as something slammed into the wing. The guns chattered on. Then, the observer jumped. His parachute blossomed out below the balloon.

Frank's tracers were pelting into the swollen skin of the balloon as he pulled out of his screaming dive. His Spad shuddered violently. Then the plane staggered as a wave of hot air hit it from the exploding balloon!

Frank righted the speeding ship and climbed for altitude at the rate of 6,500 feet in five minutes. But the controls of the plane seemed a little mushy. Tatters of wing covering began to trail in the swift rush of air. He saw a splintered strut out of the corner of his eye.

He was far above the earth when, at last, he leveled the plane and streaked for the American lines. Far below him, behind the German lines, a scarf of smoke hung in the air, slowly being raveled by the wind. Frank grinned. Let them argue about *that* victory!

But he wasn't satisfied just leaving the column of smoke in the air as a symbol of his success. He looked for American observation balloons and saw two of them hanging high in the air. He eased the shaky Spad down to a landing on a cleared field and climbed out, grinning at the shouting men who ran up to congratulate him.

"Did you see me get that baby?" he asked the group around him.

From the answers he got, there was no doubt, but what Frank Luke of Phoenix, Arizona, was on his way to becoming an ace. He collected affidavits from officers of the balloon company and went back to his plane.

The boys of the Twenty-seventh treated Frank Luke with more respect that night, but Frank hardly noticed it. He had something on his mind. He wanted to learn all he could about those German gasbags.

* * *

Frank Luke and Joe Wehner talked to veteran French pilots of a nearby *escadrille*. They learned plenty. They were told that veteran pilots usually left the bags alone unless specifically ordered to attack them. There were a number of reasons, all of them deadly.

"*Oui!*" said a French ace. "The Germans have covered the ground beneath them with antiaircraft weapons of all sorts. These guns are sited so that they have a converging fire above the balloon. There is also the *flaming onion*, which is as terrifying as it is dangerous."

An American serving with the French *escadrille* leaned close to the two young men. "Then you have something else to consider. The Germans have airfields not too far from the balloon positions, and they can get a flight of Fokkers into the air just about the time you think you have the whole sky to yourself."

"But somebody has to get them," said Luke.

"Yeah...but let somebody *else* do it, kid."

The two young men walked slowly back to their quarters that warm September night. Frank looked at Joe. "I'd like to make a specialty of getting those big sausages, Joe."

"Yeah?"

Frank nodded. "I'm not afraid of the machine guns and *flaming onions*, but I don't want a German pilot breathing tracers down my neck when I go down on the carpet after a bag."

Joe smiled in his slow way. "Well then, Frank, I'll go along to cover you."

"We'll make a team, Joe!" said Frank enthusiastically.

"Luke and Wehner, Balloon Busters, Inc."

They were quiet as they walked the rest of the way. Joe Wehner had no idea how prophetic his casual words would be.

* * *

September 14, 1918, was a bright, clear day, and the newly formed team of Luke and Wehner went aloft for a little balloon-hunting. The two Spads droned along until Joe waggled his wings and pointed to the right. A great bag hung lazily in the air near a battered French town. Luke glanced at his map. The town was Busy, or what had once been Busy. The balloon was the one they had been ordered to destroy.

Luke waved a hand to Joe. Joe began to make altitude, watching for Fokkers. Luke tilted down into a power dive, and the wind screamed through his wires.

Again, the *flaming onions* arced up to meet him. The bag got bigger and bigger, but Frank held his fire. The observer left the wicker basket and plummeted down under his parachute. Then the Vickers began to rattle, and Frank's tracers seemed to sink into the bag. Nothing happened, and Frank pulled out of his dive to skim across the fat back of the balloon while German bullets flicked through the tight fabric of wings and fuselage.

Frank looked up. Nine planes were milling about high overhead, like darting insects. One of them was Joe, and it was certain the other eight weren't Allied planes. Frank banked his Spad in a shuddering turn and came in low at almost treetop level before he lifted the blunt nose of the Spad and opened up with his machine guns. This time, the big bag gushed a huge ball of gas and flame, and the tiny Spad shot past the holocaust and clawed for altitude.

Frank craned his neck. The Fokkers were far out of position, and Joe Wehner was high above them, safe enough for the time being. As Frank Luke leveled off, he saw another balloon being hauled down near Boinville. He opened the throttle of the Spad and dived for the sinking bag.

It seemed as though he were diving into a cauldron of fire. His plane was struck again and again, and the controls became mushy. But as he banked, he opened fire, plunging hot tracers into the bag, and it blew. Frank yelled into the roaring slipstream, a real cowboy yell. *"Yippeeeee!"*

When he got out of his plane that day, he knew it would never fly again. His crew chief shook his head. "Mr. Luke," he said, "I wonder what held that crate together long enough for you to get home."

Joe Wehner came in for a landing. His Spad was well peppered with bullet holes, too, and he admitted he had downed a Fokker while protecting Frank.

* * *

Frank Luke had a fresh Spad the next day, and in company with Joe Wehner, he flew toward Boinville. Somehow, in the clouds, they became separated. Frank looked in vain for Joe, then characteristically kept on by himself. A balloon swayed in the air over Boinville, in the same place where Frank had shot one down just the day before. He flew away from the area, then turned and dropped in altitude after warming up his guns. He swept in fast, hedgehopping over trees and fields, while startled, white-faced Germans looked up from under their coal-scuttle helmets. The balloon seemed to grow swiftly in size.

The ground crew scattered for cover as the roaring Spad shot past them. Above the sound of the engine came the incessant chattering of the machine guns, and then the Spad banked away just as the bag erupted in a mass of flames and smoke. The tattered burning fragments had not settled to the ground, and the *flaming onions* and angry tracers were still chasing Frank when he banked sharply, leveled his plane, and flew at top speed toward the Bois D'hingry, hardly clearing the treetops.

The big balloon at Bois D'hingry was settling slowly as its winch hauled it down. Then a gnat of a plane roared in, sparkling with gunfire, and the tracers tucked into the distended skin of the *drachen* and sent it down. The Spad shot over the flames and climbed in a tight spiral while the grinning pilot waved down at the yelling ground crew, then vanished into the clouds.

Frank looked back over his shoulder. The sky seemed full of planes, and they weren't Allied planes. They were snub-nosed, thick-winged Fokkers, and they were out for blood—Frank Luke's blood. There was no time for him to make evasive maneuvers or try to get above and behind them. He gunned the Spad and leveled out for a race to the Allied side of the lines with the seven Fokkers streaming behind him, gun flashes sparkling from their ugly noses.

Bullets flicked past Frank's head and tore into his

instrument-panel, shattered his windscreen, and screamed viciously from the butts of his twin Vickers guns. Then suddenly, the shooting stopped. Frank risked a quick look behind him. He shouted for joy and pounded the edge of his cockpit.

A lone Spad was chasing the Fokkers, but now there were only five of them. One Fokker was plummeting down to earth, leaving a stain of smoke against the sky, while another one was whirling down minus a wing. There wasn't any doubt who was in *that* Spad. Joe Wehner had arrived right on time!

When the two young flyers landed, they were greeted by a mob of shouting squadron members. It was then that Frank learned that Joe had shot down a balloon near Verdun, then had seen the Fokkers on Frank's tail, had knocked down the two closest Germans, and had driven off the rest. The team was really in business now. Between the two of them, on two consecutive days, they had scored eight victories. Frank was now rated as an ace, having five confirmed victories since September 12, while Joe Wehner was but one victory short of being an ace.

While Frank listened to the congratulations, he was looking toward the front lines. There were more balloons over there, and he had a whole afternoon to hunt them. Hunt them he would!

He went *drachen-hunting* alone that afternoon. It seemed as though he just couldn't miss. Another balloon went down in flames. The cocky kid from Arizona had begun to come up to his big talk. Six balloons in three days of flying time. It was hard to believe. But the veteran French and American pilots shook their heads. Luke was going at it too hard. The odds were always against balloon hunters.

* * *

Luke proved them all wrong the next day, September 16. It was early evening when two Spads shot in toward a group of the big bags minutes before they were due to be hauled down. Tracers streamed through the darkening sky, and within a few minutes, there were three towering plumes of flame and smoke hanging in the evening sky as three *drachens* breathed for the last time. Joe got two of them and Frank one.

The team of Luke and Wehner, Inc., was famous now along the tangled battle lines of the American Toul and Château-Thierry sectors. Doughboys in the trenches and artillerymen hated those looming gasbags because it seemed to them that the German observers were practically looking down into their mess kits as they ate.

But there was a stubborn, headstrong streak in Frank Luke. He had an amused contempt for authority and had a habit of coming and going as he pleased, which boded no good for him. Yet, despite his insubordination and extreme self-confidence, his commanding officers had to agree that he had the ideal combination of flying ability, marksmanship, and fighting spirit to make a great ace of aces. And as the saying goes, "They hadn't seen anything yet."

September 18 was a bright fall day. The fighting team of Luke and Wehner took to the air. Their goal was three balloons near Labeuville. Frank came in low, and Joe came in high, Frank aiming for the balloons while Joe provided cover. Frank flew almost as though he planned on going right through the first balloon while a vicious curtain of Archie fire danced and smoked in front of him. His plane shuddered with hit after hit, but he saw nothing except that fat balloon.

He shot over it and heard the roaring explosion as he leveled off, banked, and then came in at the second balloon with chattering guns. It, too, went up in flames, and he splitessed upward to get away from the gunfire.

Frank had been too busy to wonder about Joe. All he knew was that he hadn't been bothered by Fokkers. He craned his neck. Seven planes were tangling in a wild melee high overhead. Six of them were marked with the black cross of the German air force, while the seventh plane was a Spad marked with the red, white, and blue of the United States Air Corps. It was Joe Wehner faithfully providing cover for Frank.

The odds evened up as Frank tore into the fight, shooting from almost impossible angles. Tracers slammed into the back of a German pilot, and his Fokker tumbled down in flames. Frank dived immediately on another Fokker and stitched a hot pattern of steel up the fuselage from tail to engine, then zoomed away from the plane as it went into the deadly tailspin.

He clawed for altitude. There was no sign of Joe Wehner in the smoky skies. Frank headed for home, but there was a terrible foreboding in him about Joe. Time and time again, he looked back, but there was no sight of his friend. Hot anger burned in Frank, as well as an intense hatred of the enemy.

Five planes were milling around in the sky over the blood-soaked battlefield of Verdun. Four of them were Spads with the French Air Service insignia on them, while the fifth was a lone German Halberstadt observation plane. The rear-gunner was giving a good account of himself, keeping the buzzing French gnats off his tail. Suddenly, another Spad shot down out of the sky, plastered the Halberstadt with machine-gun bullets, then streaked for the lines as the German plane fell off on one wing, fluttered down a few hundred feet, and burst into a ball of orange flame. Four veteran French pilots looked rather silly as they watched Frank Luke disappear in the distance.

It was dusk when Frank came in for a landing. He could see the squadron personnel standing on the field. When he left his bullet-pocked ship, a pilot yelled at him, "You really did it this time, Frank! Two balloons and three planes in about ten minutes' fighting time!"

Frank took off his goggles and helmet and felt the cool breeze blow through his damp blond hair. "What about Joe?" he asked.

None of them answered. They didn't have to speak. Frank knew that one-half of the team of Luke and Wehner, Inc. was gone forever.

There wasn't any doubt about the victory score. Practically the whole of the famous Rainbow Division had seen the balloons and planes go down. Congratulations poured in from all sides, but it was a lonely twenty-one-year-old pilot who kept to himself that night. Joe Wehner, the son of German immigrants, several times suspected because of his name, had paid with his life for Frank's five victories.

* * *

Something happened within Frank Luke after the death of Joe Wehner. He became more careless of authority than he had ever been before. Time after time, he would disobey orders, or deliberately ignore them. As often as not, he would take off from the field just about dusk on a balloon hunt, and most of the time, he was successful. He was given a leave to Paris, the goal of almost every member of the AEF, but he was back on duty long before his leave time was up.

The twenty-sixth of September was the day Frank went aloft with a new teammate, Lieutenant Ivan Roberts, a Massachusetts boy. Squadron members hoped Roberts would be able to replace Joe Wehner as top cover for Frank. It wasn't any use. Five Fokkers jumped the two Americans as they flew low on an approach attack against some balloons. Luke got a balloon, but that day, Ivan Roberts was shot down to his death.

Frank went AWOL the next day, in his plane, although he had been ordered not to leave the field. Another balloon was added to his mounting score. His record by the twenty-seventh of September was a total of eighteen balloons and planes, or an average of a little better than one a day since he had shot down that first balloon near Marieulles. It was an incredible score for such a short time of flying.

They grounded Frank Luke when he returned to his squadron, but somehow, he managed to take off in his Spad, which he landed at a forward airfield. Orders went out for his arrest. It was the twenty-ninth of September 1918. Frank took off before he could be arrested. He was truly a *lone eagle* now. Just before sunset, he flew low over the American balloon headquarters near Souilly and dropped a note: "Watch those three Hun balloons on the Meuse, Luke..."

The sky was darkening as Frank Luke flew toward Dun-sur-Meuse. He could see the huge swaying gasbags along the Meuse River. Time and again, he craned his neck, looking for enemy planes, but the sky was clear of them. He tested his guns. They rattled steadily. Thoughts of Joe Wehner and Ivan Roberts came to his mind. His hatred for the enemy seemed to settle on the bloated *drachens*.

Then began his swift, furtive flight over trees and fields, straight for the first balloon. His guns rattled, and he banked away as the first balloon flared up. The second balloon was at Briere Farm, and it, too, died violently in flame and smoke. Machine-gun, rifle, and antiaircraft fire converged on the lone Spad, and it bucked in the disturbed air while bullets cracked through the wings and fuselage.

Flaming onions sailed lazily up to meet the racing Spad.

The third balloon was at Milly, but there were two Fokkers between Frank Luke and his goal. They came in at him from each side, but there was no stopping the American. Tracers lashed out at the first plane, and it hit the ground near the Meuse.

The second Fokker shot past Luke. He didn't follow it. He flew toward the balloon. The Fokker turned, and too late, the pilot saw the blunt nose of the Spad spangled with flaming machine-gun muzzles. Bullets tore into the Fokker, and it crashed in flames.

Something had ripped through the side of the Spad and into Frank Luke's flesh, but he had enough strength to level off and fly toward the third and last of the balloons. It was being hauled down, but that didn't save it. His guns chattered, and he swept past it as it burst into flames, illuminating the country for a great distance. In the glare, Frank saw more Fokkers darting in at him like angry wasps.

The Spad was swaying from side to side now. The engine was missing, coughing and catching, then missing again. Frank shook his head. It was getting darker, and an intolerable thirst grew in him. Just ahead of him was a little French town—probably Murvaux, he thought dazedly. There were men in the street looking toward him. Men in coal-scuttle helmets and *feldgrau* uniforms. He eased the plane downward a little, caught a group of the men in his ring sights, and opened fire with the last of his ammunition. The Germans scattered, leaving half a dozen of their number lying on the ground.

The Spad was almost done for. Frank saw a fairly level field near a stream. Thirst gripped his throat with rough fingers. The staggering Spad's engine at last cut out completely. Wind whistled eerily through the wires as the battered plane floated down for its landing. It struck and bumped, then rolled to a standstill. Frank pulled himself out of the cockpit and dropped to the ground. He shook his head. There was water just ahead.

"Surrender!" a man yelled in a thick accent.

Frank felt for his holstered automatic pistol. He drew it out and pulled back the slide, letting it snap forward to load the first of seven cartridges into the chamber.

Dim figures rose from the shadows and closed in on

him. They carried rifles. "Surrender! Surrender!" one of them yelled again.

The young pilot raised his pistol and began to shoot. Then the rifles cracked. Something hit him in the chest, and Frank Luke went down forever. He didn't know the meaning of the word *surrender*.

* * *

Frank Luke was buried by French villagers in the little graveyard at Murvaux and then re-interred after the war in the American Military Cemetery at Romagne. For his gallantry in action and intrepidity beyond the call of duty, he was posthumously awarded the Medal of Honor, as well as many other American and foreign decorations. Official records vary as to how many victories he scored, but most reports give the total as twenty-one. He is rated as the second-highest-scoring ace of the United States Air Corps in World War One.

Frank Luke's combat record becomes even more incredible when compared to those of other fliers of his time. Captain Eddie Rickenbacker, top-ranking ace of the AEF, scored his twenty-six victories in seven months' flying time. Lieutenant Michel Coiffard of France scored thirty-four victories, of which twenty-eight were balloons, to become the top-ranking *balloon buster* of World War One, in twenty months of flying time. Willy Coppens of Belgium ranked second as a *balloon buster* with a score of thirty-seven victories, twenty-six of which were balloons, in sixteen months of combat. *Leutnant* Heinrich Gontermann of the German air force was the top enemy *balloon-strafer* with a total of thirty-nine victories, seventeen of them being balloons, in ten months of aerial combat. Those were all excellent records, but Frank Luke, the Arizona cowboy, made his amazing record of twenty-one victories in *seventeen days* of combat flying.

In Phoenix, Arizona, on the capital grounds there is an oversize likeness in bronze of Frank Luke standing on a granite base. Embedded in the base are replicas of five of the medals awarded to the *balloon buster*. On the reverse side of the pedestal is a bronze tablet bearing the names of the Arizona men who died in World War One.

FIVE
TERROR ON THE BLACK ISLE

HERMAN H. HANNEKEN

DISTANT FIRES SHONE like jewels through the black velvet of the Haitian night. As the wind shifted, the thudding from voodoo drums carried faintly down to the barracks of the Haitian Gendarmes in Grand Riviere. Now and then, the eerie sound of conch horns mingled with the constant drumming.

The people of Grand Riviere were afraid. They were afraid of the voodoo priests and their bloody rites, and now they were afraid of something else. Charlemagne Peralte, the powerful leader of the Cacos, had started a bloody reign of terror on the Black Island.

Herman Henry Hanneken, captain in the Haitian Gendarmery, stood in the darkness near the barracks and looked at the distant fires. Deep hatred for Charlemagne Peralte glowed within him, as bright and as hot as those faraway voodoo fires. Peralte held the Republic of Haiti enslaved by fear. He was backed by the Cacos, whose razor-edged machetes could lop off a man's arm or head with ease.

The Cacos were rebels, but there was nothing noble

about their cause. They lived to loot and kill, and their very name showed what they really were. The native Caco bird fed mainly on little lizards, just as the Cacos lived mainly from little people.

Hanneken paced back and forth. His rank in the gendarmes was a temporary one. He was really a sergeant in the First Regiment, United States Marine Corps, who had been hand-picked to train and lead the Haitian Gendarmes.

As a sergeant of Marines, he had been trained into a first-class fighting machine. The credo of the Marines is to *attack* the enemy, not to wait passively on defense.

That was what was bothering Herman Hanneken that hot night in Grand Riviere. He had never met Charlemagne Peralte, but he hated him as he had never hated any other man.

Feet crunched on the gravel, and a dark figure loomed through the darkness. It was Lieutenant Bill Button of the Gendarmes, otherwise Corporal Button, USMC.

"Still riling you, Herm?" Button asked.

Hanneken grunted. There was no need to answer. They had both been stationed in Haiti since 1915, four long, tough years, missing the action other leathernecks had seen in France during World War One. But they had had action enough. They had found other Marines in the matted, steaming jungles or on the trackless mountainsides, hacked to bits by Caco machetes.

"No trails," Button said thoughtfully. "Thousands of blood-hungry Cacos waiting up there and gathering more strength every day. How long do you think it will be before Peralte takes over the whole island?"

Hanneken smashed a fist into his other palm. "You

can kill Cacos by the hundreds," he said, "and still not break up the so-called revolution."

Bill Button nodded agreement. "So?"

Hanneken lowered his voice. "The best way to kill a snake is to cut off its head, Bill."

Button stared at his friend and commanding officer. "You feel all right, Herm? I mean, you haven't got a touch of malaria or something?"

Hanneken shook his head. "I've been thinking of a way to nail Peralte."

Button flipped away a cigarette. "Shoot!" he said.

Hanneken grinned. Quietly, he explained his plan.

Button was at first shocked at the audacity of it. But he was a marine, and he knew Hanneken would have to depend on him to make the plan work. The two tough leathernecks gripped hands in the darkness while the drums thudded on.

Hanneken lay awake on his cot that night, staring up at the dim whiteness of his mosquito netting, still hearing those drums. Haiti had been aptly called the Black Isle. Its people had been under the control of voodoo priests and would-be dictators for over a hundred years. They were confused, uneducated, hot-blooded, and ridden by superstition and fear.

The First Regiment of United States Marines had landed in Haiti in 1915 to protect United States interests after Haitian President V. Guillaume Sam had been hacked to bits in the street. They had established a relative peace, and the newly formed government had ratified a treaty to establish the Gendarmery d'Haiti, formed of native Haitians and officered by picked marine non-coms like Hanneken and Button. The two Americans and one hundred crack gendarmes had come to Grand Riviere to keep the Cacos in check. They had done pretty well, too, until Charlemagne Masena Peralte had escaped from prison with a fanatical determination to drive all whites into the sea.

Charlemagne was a *griffe,* or a person whose ancestors had been slaves to the French until the revolt of 1803, whereupon they had moved into a vacated French mansion and had lived like a wealthy family ever since. He had been well educated and had taken a law degree in France. Fierce, extremely ugly, and physically powerful, he had a brilliant, if somewhat twisted, mind.

The Caco leader had said he would be crowned Charlemagne the First, King of Haiti. But there was one major obstacle in his way, and it looked like a case of the irresistible meeting the immovable. That obstacle was Captain Herman Henry Hanneken of the Gendarmery d'Haiti.

* * *

The morning after his decision to go ahead with his dangerous plan, Hanneken talked for a long time with Bill Button. "We could chase these Cacos all over Haiti," he said as he refilled his coffee cup, "and never subdue the movement."

Button nodded. "Just like the old Indian-fighting days. They raid, then split and vanish, and if we follow them, we get ambushed."

The odds were high against the Marines. Charlemagne controlled ten thousand square miles of jungle. He kept a personal bodyguard of six or seven hundred hand-picked men, well-armed with pistols, rifles, and the ever-present, razor-sharp machete. His headquarters, wherever it happened to be at the time, was surrounded by his bodyguard, with every path and trail watched day and night. Drum-talk brought him news and sent his orders across jungle and mountain without the use of wires.

Hanneken had once posted a reward of two thousand dollars for the head of Charlemagne, but it hadn't worked. Informers were slaughtered as sacrifices in Charlemagne's bloody revival of voodooism. There was only one way to defeat Charlemagne; that was to kill or capture him and his sub-chiefs.

"I've already received permission from headquarters to try out my scheme," Hanneken said. "But we'll need help. I figured on using Sergeant Leonce Compere and Corporal Edmund Francois."

Button nodded. "Two good men."

"And I'll need one more man to make this scheme a success. I doubt if I can carry it off without him."

Button looked up. "Who is he?"

"Jean Conze."

Button whistled softly. "*Jean Conze?* He hates you, Herm!"

Hanneken grinned crookedly. "Yeah, but he hates Charlemagne worse than he does me."

"That's a fact!"

Jean Conze was a *griffe* like Charlemagne. He hated Herman Hanneken and all whites in general, but he hated Charlemagne more than any white because Charlemagne had hurt him where it hurt most, in the pocketbook. Charlemagne's Cacos had burned Conze's sugarcane fields, thus putting his very profitable sugar-refining works out of business.

Button leaned closer to Hanneken. "How do you figure on using Conze?"

"I'm going to set Conze up as a Caco."

Button stared at him. "You outta your mind?"

Hanneken shook his head. "I'm going to make Conze look real good. You know where Fort Capois is. Well, Conze is going to set up headquarters there as a Caco. When Grand Riviere learns that its most prominent citizen has become a Caco, the news will sure travel fast to Charlemagne."

"Then what happens?"

"Corporal Edmund Francois is going to desert to him, taking along a pretty good supply of Gendarmery guns and ammunition."

Button scratched his jaw. "Conze is broke. He'll need money for food, ammunition, weapons, and supplies so that he can get his Cacos. You know well enough headquarters won't finance Conze."

"No, but he'll get his money."

"Where?"

"From me, Bill. I've been on this island for four years and have saved most of my Marine and Gendarmery pay."

Button shook his head. "Man, this thing had *better* work, Herm."

* * *

And so it was. Conze went to half-ruined Fort Capois with *deserter* Edmund Francois. He boasted openly that he had good Gendarmery weapons for those who would follow the star of Jean Conze, the Caco.

Hanneken found himself in immediate trouble. His

fellow Marines and the leading citizens of Grand Riviere began to look down on him because Conze had evidently made a first-class fool out of a United States Marine. Headquarters, which had approved his scheme in general, knew nothing of the intricacies of his plan, and they began to wonder if Hanneken was as good a man as they had once thought he was. Fort Capois, as long as it was occupied by Conze and his Cacos, was a direct slap in the face to the gendarme garrison of Grand Riviere.

The drums thudded every night as Conze talked with Charlemagne across the dark miles. The gist of their conversation was that Conze wanted Charlemagne to join with him in driving the hated whites into the sea forever. Hanneken had gendarmes who knew drum-talk, and they kept him posted as to what was going on. Many of the islanders knew drum-talk, too, and the news of the proposed alliance flashed all over the Black Isle.

Charlemagne was safe on a mountain peak forty miles south of Grand Riviere, and he was not impressed with Conze's offers. To spark the leader into action, Hanneken made a fake raid on Fort Capois. There was a lot of shooting and shouting, but no damage was done, except to Hanneken's reputation when Conze drove off the gendarmes. News of this local *success* was sent immediately to Charlemagne, but still, the wily Caco chief did not bite.

In September, Hanneken staged another phony raid on Fort Capois. Hundreds of bullets sang through the air and cut creepers and vines or thudded into trees. Once again, Conze *drove off* the gendarmes. This time, Hanneken wore a bloody bandage on his left arm as he came out of the hot jungle, a defeated man. He was in disgrace with the people of Grand Riviere, but far worse, he was in disgrace with his fellow Marines who felt that he had let the Corps down. None of them knew the bloody bandage covered a good arm without a scratch on it.

Hanneken played his part well, becoming more morose and sour every day, favoring his *wounded* arm and listening to the distant thudding of the drums as Conze talked again with Charlemagne. Conze was an important man because of his two successful fights with the gendarmes. Now he was boldly asking Charlemagne to join him in a raid on Grand Riviere.

Charlemagne began to get interested. He fancied himself quite a military genius, and it was obvious that this man Conze would make a good ally. He could always get rid of him when he was no longer useful.

Charlemagne sent his *Secretary of War*, General Papillon, and seventy-five tough Cacos to consult with Conze. Papillon was to test Conze's loyalty to Charlemagne. Then Charlemagne himself, with the swiftness of sudden death, showed up at Fort Capois.

* * *

In the pitch darkness of the Haitian night, Hanneken met Jean Conze. The planter was scared half out of his wits, but he seemed willing to go ahead with the plan.

"How did you get out of Fort Capois?" asked Hanneken suspiciously.

Conze grinned. "I told Charlemagne that my rich brother wanted to help finance the revolution. The thought of money was enough to let Charlemagne allow me to leave Fort Capois."

"So how do you expect to get back? Your brother won't help you."

The dark eyes studied the big marine. "No, my friend, but perhaps *you* can?"

Hanneken bit his lip. He had one thousand dollars left in his kitty.

Conze shrugged. "However, if you do not have the money..."

Hanneken took his wallet from his shirt pocket and counted out the money. If this didn't work...

Conze swiftly folded the bills and stowed them away. He wiped the sweat from his face. "Charlemagne plans an attack on Cap Haitien prison."

Hanneken stared at the *griffe*. "That's madness! What can he hope to gain by that?"

Conze spat. "He says he will do it if only to destroy the prison in which he was once held. The man is mad!"

Hanneken leaned against a tree. "Will he listen to your advice?"

The broad face split into a wide grin. "He thinks I am a great soldier because of your defeats, *capitaine*."

Hanneken nodded. "Then convince him he must split up his forces and make several attacks at the same time. You must let me know where and when he plans these attacks."

"Yes."

"Goodbye, then, and good luck, Jean."

* * *

In a few days, the message came from Conze. It told of Charlemagne's plans. Hanneken contacted marine headquarters and revealed the time and place of each attack, warning the marine commanding officer to be ready but not to make the defense look obvious. The rat was not yet in the trap.

The sun was beating down on Grand Riviere when Hanneken and Button met with Sergeant Leonce Compere and ten other trusted gendarmes. Hanneken informed them that he needed them for a highly dangerous mission. Not one man backed out.

Later, Button spoke quietly to Hanneken. "Suppose one of these men we picked out is a traitor?"

Hanneken withdrew the cleaning rod from his favorite pistol and peered into the shining barrel. "That's a chance we have to take, Bill."

Button shrugged. "I guess you're right, Herm."

Slowly and carefully, the Marines got ready for Charlemagne. Garrisons were reinforced. Ambushes were prepared. Near Cap Haitien, 350 tough leathernecks waited in ambush, itching to get Charlemagne and his Cacos in their sights.

Conze, still playing his part, got his Cacos ready for an all-out attack on Grand Riviere.

Messengers crept into Grand Riviere in the dead of the night to keep Hanneken posted as to Charlemagne's whereabouts. This wasn't always easy to report, for the wily Caco chief shifted his headquarters here and there at odd times of the day or night. Hanneken and Button, with eleven veteran gendarmes, were ready with weapons and disguises, waiting for the word from Conze.

The word came through from Corporal Edmund

Francois, still playing his part as a gendarme deserter, now a trusted Caco lieutenant to Jean Conze. Conze was on the march to attack Grand Riviere with his men.

This was the first break. If Charlemagne had decided to let one of his own generals lead the attack, it would have led to bloodshed. As it was, Conze could be depended upon to halt at the first fire from the garrison of Grand Riviere.

"And what about Charlemagne?" asked Hanneken.

The gendarme shrugged. "He is moving his headquarters to Mazaire now. There is a certain path he must follow to get there. You understand?"

"Yes." The captain eyed him.

"I will tell Sergeant Compere how to find it." Hanneken nodded. He watched the gendarme vanish into the dark jungle. The time had come.

* * *

One by one, the gendarmes donned the ragged clothing and battered straw hats of the Cacos and drifted into the jungle to the rendezvous. It was easy enough for them—they were native Haitians—but for Hanneken and Button, it was quite another matter. They coated their faces and hands with lampblack and cold cream, pulled straw hats down low on their light hair, and then covered themselves with long ponchos.

Hanneken strapped on two pistols, one of them a heavy forty-five-caliber Colt automatic, the other a thirty-eight-caliber Colt revolver. Button concealed his Browning Automatic Rifle, more commonly called a BAR, under his poncho. That was quite a feat because the weapon weighed sixteen pounds when empty and it now contained a box magazine with twenty rounds of .30/06 cartridge in it. Button was an expert with the BAR, and he didn't intend to tangle with a few hundred bloodthirsty Cacos without the automatic rifle to even up the odds a little.

The thirteen fighting men met at the rendezvous and moved to the ambush on the trail Charlemagne was supposed to take. Time passed. Then, the wind carried the sound of firing from Grand Riviere. Hanneken bit his lip. "That's Conze's attack," he said.

Still no Charlemagne. The jungle was quiet except for the distant sounds of shooting. Then something rustled in the brush, and thirteen guns turned as one.

"*Capitaine* Hanneken," came the soft voice of Corporal Edmund Francois. He stepped out of the brush. "Things are not well," he said breathlessly. "Charlemagne decided at the last minute not to come to Mazaire until after Grand Riviere and Cap Haitien have been taken."

Hanneken smashed a fist into his other palm. Months of hard work gone for nothing! "Is he at Fort Capois?" he asked.

"No! We were told to send all messages to the fort, but his own men will carry the message to him on the great hill beyond the fort."

There was a deathly quiet in the little clearing. Hanneken looked in the direction of Fort Capois. They *might* get there. They *might* even get Charlemagne. *But would they get out?* "Can you take me there, Francois?" he asked the corporal.

Francois swallowed hard. "I know the way," he admitted slowly, "but there are six outposts on the only trail."

Hanneken did not hesitate. "Let's go!" he snapped. He followed the gendarme through the darkness to the trail, never looking back. Button shifted his BAR, then followed Hanneken. The eleven gendarmes looked at each other for a moment, then followed Button.

Francois was in the lead, walking swiftly although it was almost pitch dark, then suddenly he stopped. Guns were raised and cocked. Hanneken wet his lips as he peered into the darkness and dropped his hands to his pistol butts.

Francois moved ahead a little, then turned. "It is all right, *Capitaine*. Look!"

A mule stood in a little clearing. He brayed once, but Francois quickly quieted him. Hanneken looked on the ground. Demijohns were scattered about on the soft earth. He picked up one of them, uncorked it, and sniffed. The rich, powerful odor of rum almost made his head swim.

Francois rubbed his jaw. "Cacos were here," he said, "on their way to Grand Riviere."

"This is luck," said Hanneken.

"How so?" asked Button curiously.

Sergeant Compere grinned. "Rum is as good as a password among the Cacos," he said knowingly.

"Load the rum onto the mule," said Hanneken. "Charlemagne will be eager to hear news about the attack on Grand Riviere. Suppose we pretend we are men sent back by Conze to tell Charlemagne of a great victory." He slapped one of the demijohns. "The spoils of victory!"

Button nodded. He looked about at the men. "Act like you've been drinking some of the spoils," he said.

They left the clearing with the mule trotting

placidly along with them. Hour after hour, they kept on until by two o'clock in the morning, they had passed Fort Capois and had taken the trail that led toward Charlemagne's temporary headquarters. They stopped for a breather, and Francois came close to Hanneken. "Perhaps it would be wiser to take to the brush, *Capitaine?*"

Hanneken shoved back his hat and looked at the wall of brush and trees. "We wouldn't last five minutes in there without being lost," he said quietly. "No, Francois, it's the trail or nothing."

They marched on, and in a few minutes, there was a movement in the brush beside the trail. "Halt! Who goes there?" rang out the challenge.

The gendarmes stopped. "General Jean!" called out Francois. That had been the password earlier in the day. If it had been changed...

There was a moment's hesitation. Hanneken drew a pistol while Button threw back his poncho and gripped his BAR.

"Pass," said the sentry.

A fire glowed farther up the trail. Forty Cacos stood there, holding their rifles and razor-edged machetes. A sergeant eyed Francois. "Who are you?" he demanded suspiciously.

"One of Conze's men. This man"—Francois pointed to Hanneken—"is General Bias of General Conze's army. We bring news to Charlemagne of a great victory at Grand Riviere!"

The sergeant eyed the rum jugs on the mule. Hanneken spoke in thick back-hills *patois,* bragging of his part in the victory. A rum jug was passed about among the guards. Still, they hesitated. Another jug was sent among them.

"We had better go on and tell the great news to Charlemagne," said Hanneken at last.

The sergeant wiped his mouth. "Only two men can go up the trail at one time," he said firmly.

"But I am General Bias!" said Hanneken. "These men are my personal bodyguard!"

"Two men at a time," insisted the sergeant.

More rum was passed, and finally, the whole party was allowed to continue up the steep trail. They wasted no time in getting away from that dangerous clearing.

Another fire winked through the dark night, and the party came to a halt. "General Jean," said Hanneken in answer to the sharp challenge.

Once again, the rum was put to work, but this outpost was tougher than the first one. "Two men at a time," said the Caco in charge. "No more!"

Hanneken blustered and acted the part of General Bias to the deep admiration of his men. "Send a messenger to the great Charlemagne," he said importantly. "Tell him it is the great General Bias, the hero of Grand Riviere, who wishes to see him."

The messenger was duly dispatched. Minutes ticked past while the gendarmes lounged about the fire, with Button and Hanneken keeping as far away from the light as possible. In thirty minutes, the Caco came back. It was all right. Charlemagne the First would see the *heroes of Grand Riviere*.

The gendarmes began the long climb up the steep trail. They reached the edge of the jungle. The summit of the steep hill had been cleared of trees and brush. A fire winked through the darkness. Four sentries barred the way at the edge of the jungle. By their fine uniforms and splendid weapons, Hanneken knew they must be Charlemagne's personal bodyguard.

"Two men may pass, my general," one of them said. "Yourself and one other. No more."

Edmund Francois stepped forward and was recognized as one of General Jean Conze's staff. "He may go, too," said the leader of the guards.

Hanneken, Button, and Francois walked forward toward the fire. The rich odor of coffee wafted toward them. A large group of Caco officers stood about the fire, and an old woman crouched beside a cauldron. The firelight revealed the partly vine-covered ruins of an old fort behind the officers.

Then Hanneken saw him. There was no mistaking that bestial, froglike face, even as Francois spoke out of the side of his mouth. "It is Charlemagne," he said quietly.

It was very quiet as the three men approached. The old woman glanced up, then poked the fire. Wood flared up brightly, and the light revealed the startling blue eyes of Herman Hanneken in contrast to the heavy coating of lampblack.

One of the officers shouted, but the old crone thought the quickest of all of them. She dumped over the cauldron into the fire. Steam hissed, and bright ember eyes winked up in the sudden darkness. Some of the light was reflected from the pearl-handled pistol Charlemagne had drawn. It was enough of a target for Herman Hanneken as he whipped out his thirty-eight-caliber pistol and emptied it at the dim shadow of Charlemagne. He knew he had not missed.

Hanneken jumped backward, clawing for his forty-five as pistols cracked flatly from the area near the fire.

Bill Button stood to one side with his BAR at hip level. He cut loose at full automatic, and the chattering of the heavy weapon drowned all other noise.

The BAR seemed to chew away through the shrieking Caco officers. Some of them went down, and others dived for shelter. Powder smoke drifted across the clearing to mingle with the smoke from the fire, and guns flashed as the Cacos got up courage again when the BAR stopped. But it had stopped only long enough for Button to rip out the empty magazine and ram home a loaded one. Once again, the leaping, stabbing tongues of orange-red flame lighted up the clearing.

* * *

Sergeant Compere had acted swiftly. The four bodyguards died under gendarme guns as soon as Hanneken opened fire on Charlemagne. Then Compere and his shouting gendarmes charged toward Hanneken, Button, and Francois, who were fighting a one-sided battle. The gendarmes plunged into the brushy hollow where the three others were shooting. Rifles began to speak. Every time a Caco gun flashed, a scythe of cupro-nickel bullets would sweep over the spot. If the firing of the Cacos got too heavy, Button would touch off the BAR until it was almost too hot for him to handle. It made all the difference in odds of ten to one because the Cacos couldn't stand that chattering devil of a gun and the grinning marine who handled it so well.

There was a lull in the firing. Hanneken inched forward.

"Where you going, Herm?" asked Button.

"To get Charlemagne."

"You're loco!"

But Hanneken bellied along until he saw Cacos moving about, and then he boldly stood up and walked among them, depending on his disguise to save him, until he saw the sprawled body of Charlemagne the First. He picked up the body, slung it over his shoulder, and walked back to the hollow. All about him, he could hear shouting, cursing Cacos blundering through the brush, shooting at each other as well as at the gendarmes.

The shooting died away for a time, only to break out in sporadic outbursts, which were answered by the gendarmes. It was close to dawn when Button emptied a magazine and then shoved a full one into the BAR. "That's the last of the lot," he said dryly. "Twenty rounds."

The gendarmes looked at each other. Ammunition was low. There were a lot of Cacos out in the brush.

"Listen!" said Leonce Compere sharply.

They could hear men yelling down along the trail.

"Reinforcements," said Edmund Francois. He opened and closed the bolt of his rifle.

"Wait!" said Hanneken.

The false dawn was tinting the eastern sky, and a cool wind swept across the summit of the hill.

The gendarmes began to distinguish words now and then. Compere looked at Hanneken. "They say they were beaten back by Marines...that the Marines are hot after them. They are pulling out, I think, *Capitaine*."

They crouched in the hollow, resting on their weapons, waiting and watching. Now and then, they heard a shot, or the distant blowing of a conch horn. By the time the sun was up, the gendarmes seemed alone on the hilltop. The bodies of Cacos lay scattered about in their gaudy finery.

Hanneken and Button slowly closed in on the ruins. They counted nine dead Caco leaders. Button stood guard with his BAR while Hanneken rummaged through the *headquarters*. He found confidential and informative portfolios, but best of all, he found a list of Charlemagne's spies who were posted in high government places.

Compere scouted the trail and came back to report that not a live Caco was in sight. They loaded the squat, lifeless hulk of Charlemagne the First onto the rum-toting mule. Even in death, Charlemagne was hard to handle, for he kept slipping underneath the mule's belly until Hanneken ripped a door from a hut, captured four Caco stragglers, and made them carry the body of their late chief down to Grand Riviere.

* * *

There was one more thing to do to make sure the rebellion was broken forever. Too many times in the past, Caco leaders had been killed, only to have new ones springing up in their places, claiming they had not been killed at all. To prevent a *resurrection* of Charlemagne, public funerals were held in the five major cities of Haiti so that the people would know he was truly dead. It was gruesome but effective. Later, the body was buried in secret under the concrete steps of the entrance to the Department Headquarters of the North, where a sentry stands guard day and night.

Herman Henry Hanneken was field promoted to second lieutenant, United States Marine Corps, and together with Corporal Bill Button, he was awarded the Medal of Honor, as well as the *Medaille Militaire* of the Haitian Government. In time, Hanneken even got back the money he had *invested* in the Conze *revolution*.

The award of the Medal of Honor in peacetime is a rarity in itself, but the story of Herman Henry Hanneken did not stop there in Haiti in 1919. He returned to the States after Bill Button died of malaria. As Lieutenant-Colonel Hanneken in World War Two, he fought at Guadalcanal, Peleliu, and Cape Gloucester. For his heroism in combat there and in other operations, he was awarded the Navy Cross, the Legion of Merit, and the Bronze Star. In all the heat of combat in the Pacific theatre of operations, he must sometimes have thought of that dark night in the jungles of Haiti when he won the Medal of Honor against incredible odds.

SIX
TOO YOUNG TO FIGHT!
AUDIE MURPHY

THE BIG MARINE recruiting sergeant looked up at the thin face of the kid in front of the desk. "How old are you?" he asked.

"Eighteen, sir!"

"Yep," the sergeant said dryly. His experienced eyes studied the thin frame of the young Texas boy. "How tall?" he asked at last.

"Five feet seven, Sergeant."

The sergeant nodded, then looked the kid full in the eyes. "How much do you weigh?"

The kid hesitated. "One hundred and eight pounds, sir."

The sergeant shook his head. "You can't make the US Marines. Try the Army down the street. I hear they have a war on, too." He turned away to avoid the hurt look in the kid's eyes.

The boy walked toward the door.

"What did you say your name was?" called out the sergeant.

The kid turned. "Murphy...Audie Murphy..." Then he was gone.

The sergeant shrugged. He had to face many of these boys trying to worm their way into the Marines. The Marines wanted men. "Audie Murphy," he said with a grunt, then promptly dismissed the episode from his mind. It wasn't until three or four years later that he would remember that name with a start...*Audie Murphy*.

* * *

The kid had a hard time. He was seventeen, not eighteen, in that blazing war year of 1942, and he wanted to be a marine, a flier, or a soldier—anything so that he could get away from the cotton fields of his part of Texas. But the paratroopers turned him down, too, although an experienced recruiting sergeant tipped the boy off to fill up on bananas and milk. It was a good tip. He made four pounds that way and was finally accepted in the infantry.

It didn't take him long to get a nickname in his training outfit at Camp Wolters, Texas. Service outfits have a neat way of tabbing a man with a nickname that sticks. For thirteen weeks of basic training, the skinny sharecropper's kid was called *Baby*.

* * *

In August of 1944, units of the Third Division, Seventh United States Army, landed at Yellow Beach in the invasion of southern France. Company B of the

Fifteenth United States Infantry was pinned down by accurate enemy machine-gun fire soon after they had landed. The German machine guns were on a wooded hill with command of the vineyards and canebrakes where Baker Company had taken cover. The murderous fire ripped through the canes and trees. "Medic! Medic! *Medic!*" rose from dust-hoarse voices in the canes.

Baker Company was truly held up and they couldn't go back. A young staff sergeant ran his M1 carbine dry, then realized he needed a lot more firepower than he had. He crawled back to a light machine gun and dragged it forward. There was only one place to set up the machine gun for accurate fire on the enemy guns. Out in the open. The non-com dashed out, set up the gun, sighted quickly, and opened fire, stitching a row of bullets along the rim of the enemy position. The enemy fire died away.

"Come on!" yelled the young sergeant. He ran forward and opened fire with his carbine. One of his men followed and hurled grenades until he was killed. Then the sergeant began throwing them. When the smoke cleared, the young non-com was master of the hill, and B Company advanced.

The sergeant was a hard-bitten veteran of the fighting in Sicily. He had been in the bitter fighting near Salerno, and he had fought along the bloody Volturno River. At Anzio, which almost ended in the Germans driving the Americans back into the sea, he gained his staff sergeancy and command of a platoon of veterans, and later, he led them on the advance to Rome. He was just a few months past his nineteenth birthday when he brought his platoon ashore at Yellow Beach. His name was Murphy...Audie Murphy...

The Seventh Army drove on toward the Vosges Mountains after the landings in southern France. Of an original complement of 235 officers and men in B Company, Fifteenth Infantry, Third Division, which had landed in North Africa early in 1943, there were only a few originals left. Audie Murphy, who had joined in time for the Sicilian invasion, ranked as one of its veterans.

The tough young combat soldier had learned to be a scrapper at an early age. Born in a sharecropper's cabin near Farmersville, Texas, on June 20, 1925, he was one of eleven children crowded into a four-room shack with the father and mother. In 1939, the father deserted his ailing wife and eleven children and never came back.

Audie became the family mainstay, borrowing a twenty-two-caliber rifle with which to hunt rabbits. When he didn't have cartridges, he used a slingshot. He worked at a variety of jobs.

His mother died in 1941, and two of his sisters and one of his brothers were placed in an orphanage. While Audie was stationed at Camp Wolters, he sent every spare dime back to the orphanage. After basic training, he was shipped to Fort George G. Meade, Maryland, for fourteen more weeks of training, and there continued a private war between Audie Murphy and his well-wishers. He was so slight and baby-faced that his officers seemed to want to protect him.

At Camp Wolters, they had tried to ship him to Cooks and Bakers School, but he fought the idea. At Fort Meade, they tried to get him assigned as part of the permanent force, but he wiggled out of that. They placed him in the Post Exchange as a clerk, but somehow, young Murphy managed to land in North Africa as an infantry replacement for the Third Division.

In the months that followed, Audie had seen many comrades get killed or seriously wounded. But somehow, despite his always being in the very thick of the fighting, he managed to avoid the fate of his comrades. In those months, he became skilled with a Tommy gun, Garand rifle, M1 carbine, Browning Automatic Rifle, and all the other lethal tools the modern infantryman uses in the pursuit of his deadly trade.

He wasn't always lucky in the strictest sense. A mortar shell had exploded between his feet in France, and the concussion had knocked him out and broken the carbine in his hands. But, even then, his only real injury was a wound in the heel.

*** * ***

The weather had turned cold. The Germans were masters of the art of the slow, stubborn retreat, and the Third Division had suffered heavily. The terrain was thickly wooded, and though frost was thick on the ground every morning, during the day, General Mud took over, and units had to plow through the icy gumbo.

Audie's company had been in the thick of it. One day, he was called back to regimental headquarters, where he and two other bearded non-coms were field promoted to second lieutenants. The officer who promoted them shook their hands, smiled, and told them, "You are now *gentlemen* by Act of Congress. Shave, take a bath, then get back into the lines."

Later, after three days of tough fighting through

endless woods and fields, Second Lieutenant Audie Murphy was leading a B Company platoon. The dawn had been cold, and the October day was raw. The American artillery had opened up with a roaring, walking barrage behind which the Third Division was to advance. Lieutenant Murphy led his men off the trail, and as he did so, a rifle cracked flatly, and his walkie-talkie radioman, who was only a few feet away, fell with a bullet hole just above the left eye.

"Sniper!" yelled Murphy as he jumped for cover, a fraction too late. A red-hot iron slammed against his hip.

Audie raised his carbine. There was a slight movement as a camouflage covering was lifted from a foxhole. The carbine spat flame, and the sniper was dead.

Bad weather had slowed Murphy's journey to the hospital, and when he got there, the doctor found that gangrene had set in. It had cost Audie several pounds of infected flesh, which he could ill afford to spare, but in time, he had recovered. He was needed in the line. The mortality in combat officers was terribly high.

* * *

The dull light of dawn spread across the woods and fields near Holtzwihr, France, on the morning of January 26, 1945. There was a gloomy, foreboding look about the woods. The black-etched tree trunks and branches stood out against the knee-deep snow. An icy wind swept down from the Vosges Mountains and cut through thick woolen clothing.

Audie's B Company had been given orders to, "Drive to the edge of the woods facing Holtzwihr, dig in...*and hold.*" They had reached the edge of the woods facing Holtzwihr, all right, but digging into the frozen earth was another matter. And there was yet another part of the order to be filled...*to hold the ground.*

Audie stamped back and forth. It was no place for a warm-blooded Texas boy. He could hear the men muttering. They didn't know the grand strategy of war —nor did he, for that matter. An infantryman's field of vision is limited from one ditch to another, one tree trunk to the next, one empty clip of ammunition to the next loaded one. But it was clear that the veteran Third Division was having one of the hardest fights of its distinguished career.

They had reached the Rhine, and beyond the Rhine was Germany. Some American units had already crossed that famous river. But the job of the Third Division was to eliminate the Colmar Pocket, a strongly fortified area reaching south to the Swiss border. The Colmar Pocket was a constant menace to the American advance.

The Germans knew their business. They were posted in easily defensible positions with fine fields of fire. They had plenty of armor and had the advantage of being on the defensive.

Audie called battalion headquarters at dawn. "Where is our support?" he asked.

"It will be up. Hang on. The attack will be delayed."

Audie studied the cold woods, and he didn't like what he saw. Holtzwihr was about a mile off across the fields. The church steeple showed up like a thin finger against the dull sky. Beside the road leading toward Holtzwihr were the two tank destroyers which had moved up during the night. Audie walked over to them and banged on the side of one of them.

"Hey! Rise and shine! You'd better get these tin cans off the road! It's getting light! They'll blast you if you don't!"

An officer stuck his head out. "If we move into those woods, we'll get bogged down," he growled.

"You haven't any cover!"

The officer yawned. "Maybe so, but we sure have a fine field of fire."

Audie shrugged and walked over to his machine-gun squad. "How's your ammo?" he asked the sergeant.

"Four hundred rounds, maybe."

Audie whistled and shrugged. "Don't miss, Sarge."

It was lonely there in the woods as the light grew. A lone artillery observer showed up, blue with cold. Audie rubbed his unshaven jaw and rang up headquarters again. "What's the scoop?" he asked.

"No change. Hang on."

"Yeah...hang on..."

The long morning dragged by.

Suddenly, there was a rushing, whining noise in the air. The German barrage roared in, throwing up murderous clods of frozen earth, knocking out the machine-gun crew, hitting the first of the tank destroyers, killing three of the crew while the rest of them poured out of the smoking TD.

Six tanks rumbled out of the town. They split up into sections of three each. One section disappeared into the woods on one side of the road, and the other vanished into the woods on the other side.

Audie whistled softly. "Here they come. Trying to flank us from both sides."

White dots began to move across the snowy fields toward the American lines. German infantry wearing white snow capes!

The second tank destroyer kicked over its engine, and the unexpected roaring startled some of the newer men close by. The gears were meshed, and then the heavy vehicle slid helplessly into a ditch. The angle of the stranded vehicle made the guns useless. The crew wasted no time. They abandoned the helpless TD.

The artillery observer raised his head. "I can't get headquarters yet!" he called out.

Audie waved him back. "Pull out of here with that radio! I'll contact the artillery by phone!"

Audie had done artillery spotting before. He checked his map, estimated the enemy position, and then rang the field phone.

"Get me the artillery!" he snapped. "We're being attacked! Six tanks and a couple hundred infantry!"

The American artillery opened up with smoke shells and then added high explosives, square on the German lines, scattering them like duckpins. Smoke drifted through the shattered trees. Audie stared down the road and then reached for the phone just as it rang.

"How close are they?" came the question.

Audie told them to keep firing between the Americans and the advancing enemy. Then the German tanks crashed through the woods and opened up almost at point-blank range on the outnumbered Americans.

Audie cupped his hands about his mouth. "B

Company pull out! We can't stop that armor with small arms! Pull out!"

The men began to drift back. Out of 128 men and seven officers who had entered those woods at the start of the drive, there were only forty men and one officer left...Audie Murphy.

"What about you, sir?" yelled a non-com.

Audie jerked an arm, pointing to the rear. "I'll stay with the phone as long as I can. Git!"

The battered company slowly pulled back, leaving the scattered bodies of their comrades lying on the bloody snow. Audie called in some artillery corrections, then put down the phone to pick up his carbine. The Germans were a hundred yards or more from him. He shot carefully and began to drop one of the enemy after the other. It was too hot, though, for one lone American. Audie began to fall back, and then he noticed the burning TD. A machine gun was mounted on it. He glanced back over his shoulder. The German tanks had veered off.

The phone rang. "How close are they?" came the dry voice.

Audie spoke quickly. "Just hold the phone and I'll let you talk to one of them!" He carried the field phone with him, dragging the wire after it until he reached the TD. He pulled the dead body of an officer from the burning vehicle. Then he jumped to the machine gun. It looked all right, and there was plenty of ammunition. Audie cut loose with it at the line of advancing infantry. The heavy slugs chewed through the line and broke it.

Something swished through the air, and the TD seemed to ring like a bell. A direct hit! And another one!

The phone rang again. Audie mouthed corrections into it. Then he threaded a fresh belt into the machine gun and opened up again. Smoke from the burning TD was so thick he could hardly see through it. But the smoke helped, for the bewildered enemy could not tell where the fire was coming from. Audie did not realize at the time that the tanks and infantrymen of the German forces were afraid of the gas and ammunition in the TD. If the flames reached them...

The wind shifted, and Audie saw a group of Germans crouched in the roadside ditch trying to figure out where he was. They found out too late. When the machine gun stopped firing, they were all dead.

He reached for the phone. "Correct fire, battalion. Fifty over," he barked.

"Are you all right, Lieutenant?" came the anxious question.

"I'm all right, Sergeant. What are *your* postwar plans?"

In a moment, the American artillery opened up on the new range Audie had given them, and the woods became a nightmare of crashing shells, flying tree trunks, and dense smoke. Audie stared through the smoke. The German tanks had had enough. They were lumbering angrily back toward Holtzwihr, but the infantry was still in the woods and advancing along the road, practically on top of the burning TD where Audie held his phone. He raised the phone.

"Correct fire: fifty over; keep firing for effect. This is my last change."

"But that's *your* position!"

"*Fifty over,* Sergeant!"

It didn't take long. Audie Murphy's position was

soon the center of his own barrage, and the Germans broke completely.

Audie shook his head. The concussion had been terrible, and something warm was running down his right leg. He had been hit by German mortar fire. He dropped from the TD and limped through the woods, all alone. He found the company, reorganized it, and then started right back through the woods with them in a savage counterattack. Later, he called in artillery corrections, and the accurate fire did the rest.

* * *

On the plane that carried Lieutenant Audie Murphy back to the United States, he was the only junior officer among fourteen generals. But he had four rows of medals and campaign ribbons.

The sharecropper's kid from Farmersville, Texas, was famous. Among his twenty-three decorations, he had the Medal of Honor, the Distinguished Service Cross, the Silver Star with two clusters signifying that he had won that decoration three times, the Bronze Star, the Legion of Merit, and the Purple Heart with two clusters indicating that he had been wounded three times. He had been personally decorated by General De Lattre De Tassigny of France with the Legion of Honor and the *Croix de Guerre*. He was World War Two's most decorated soldier at the age of twenty years.

The Fifteenth United States Infantry of which Audie Murphy was a member during World War II had been stationed in China for many years. On the lower half of their colorful regimental insignia, they have a coiled Chinese dragon, and below the dragon is the motto *Can Do*. Audie must have remembered that motto as he stood alone in the wrecked and burning tank destroyer near Holtzwihr, France, and watched six enemy tanks and over two hundred enemy infantrymen closing in on him.

"*Can Do!*"

SEVEN
"GO IN AND GET THEM!"
SAMUEL D. DEALEY, JR

THE SMOOTH WATERS of the Sibutu Passage purled softly back from the sleek shark-nose of the fleet-type submarine USS *Harder*. Commander Samuel David Dealey, Jr. stood on his narrow and wet little bridge, staring into the darkness.

Sibutu Passage, a narrow strait between the island of Borneo and Tawi Tawi, the southernmost portion of the Philippine Islands, was no place for a United States Navy submarine. It was shallow, with clear water, and Nipponese destroyers and patrol craft, as well as patrol planes, could easily spot the slim silhouette of an enemy submarine.

But the radarman, below in the big sub, had picked up a lot of pips on his screen while the *Harder* had been submerged...three large pips and three smaller ones about twelve miles from the *Harder*. It was a convoy, and in those waters, there wasn't any doubt who *they* were. Dangerous as it was, the *Harder's* conning tower had arisen dripping from the depths, and speed had been increased to twenty knots, almost as though the veteran sub could smell her prey out there in the tropical darkness.

Four sharp-eyed lookouts hung against the steel rings of their stations and scanned the sea through night glasses. Constant reports came up from the radarman. Contact was still excellent. The bridge was quiet. No one spoke. The soft rushing of the water and the steady throbbing of the big engines were all that could be heard. Now and then, the moon sailed out from behind clouds and lighted up the dangerous passage with a silvery wash.

"I see them, sir!" a lookout called down. "Dead ahead!"

Glasses were swung and focused on those mysterious shapes. Slowly, silhouettes emerged from the darkness. "A tanker, sir," reported a lookout.

"Three," said Sam Dealey quietly.

There was a pause, and then an officer standing beside Sam Dealey said softly, "Destroyers. Three of *them* too, Skipper."

The officer knew Sam Dealey and what he was thinking. "Those tankers must be mighty important, Skipper. One *tin can* to one tanker. Top priority stuff."

Dealey merely grunted. He peered into the darkness. Destroyers were to be avoided, for a submarine was hardly a match for them. "Last patrol, we got the destroyer *Ikazuchi*," he said quietly.

The officer swallowed. He could almost feel the tension mounting in the men about them. "Not that it's any of my business," he said dryly, "but subs like *Harder* are a lot less than a match for *one* tin can, let alone *three*."

Dealey rested his arms on the edge of the bridge,

eyeing those dim shapes. One fact stuck in his racing mind, to the exclusion of all others: *The Imperial Japanese Navy was desperately short of destroyers.* Without those important war vessels to escort merchantmen, tankers, and troop transports, the lumbering cargo and transport vessels would be helpless to defend themselves against United States submarines.

Sam rubbed his jaw. He wanted those destroyers. The *Ikazuchi* sunk on the last patrol had whetted his appetite for the nasty, waspish vessels. There was only one clear answer for a fighting Texan: *Go in and get them!*

The gap between the submarine and the *Harder* had closed to about six miles, and still, Dealey did not speak. Then the moon sailed mercilessly out from behind the clouds to reveal the low silhouette of the submarine. As though it had been a signal, one of the destroyers heeled over in a sharp turn and started for the *Harder*.

"Clear the bridge! Take her down!" commanded Dealey.

The bridge was cleared, and the *Harder* slid beneath the water with a gurgling rush while the bell clanged for battle stations.

"Up periscope!"

The glistening metal shaft of the periscope slid noiselessly upward, and Commander Dealey pressed his forehead to the sponge-rubber eyepiece and draped his arms over the training handles to rotate the instrument.

"Down periscope!"

Minutes ticked by as the deadly undersea vessel was maneuvered by the skilled crew of eight officers and seventy-five enlisted men, all specialists and hand-picked men.

"Up periscope!"

The stalking began in earnest. Bearings and ranges were fed into the TDC or Torpedo Data Computer, a device for deriving a torpedo fire-control solution from data fed into it on the target's course, range, and speed. This information would be combined with data on the submarine's course and speed, and the speed of the torpedo itself.

"Down periscope! After room, make ready the after tubes. Open outer doors in after room! Up periscope!"

The big steel fish moved without fuss through the water. "Mark," said Sam Dealey. Range and bearings were instantly read off to be fed into the TDC.

"Stand by to fire...steady now...*steady*! Fire one! Fire two! Fire three!"

Three torpedoes hissed from the stern stingers of the *Harder,* and the big submarine shuddered a little. The crewmen glanced at each other, mentally ticking off the seconds.

There was a dull thud and then another a second later, followed by two thunderous explosions. Two hits out of three was top-hole shooting.

Sam Dealey had no expression on his face as he watched through the periscope. The first torpedo had struck the bow of the enemy destroyer, and the second hit had driven through the thin plating of the tin can just below the bridge. The tremendous force of the two explosions lifted the slender vessel from the water, and it fell back, sending a series of white-crested waves rushing off. Smoke arose from the doomed vessel. It sank deeper.

Dealey allowed his executive officer, and Captain, Murray T. Tichenor, Operations Officer, Submarines Seventh Fleet, to see the dying craft. The stern was rising sharply as the bows dipped down. White-uniformed men were going over the sides.

The end came quickly. She broke in half. In a few minutes, there was nothing left on the smooth surface of Sibutu Passage except floating debris, a few struggling men, and a huge oil slick spreading faster and faster. The oil slick was the impermanent grave-marker of the fifteen-hundred-ton destroyer *Minatsuki*.

The crew didn't have a chance to see the swift end of the tin can, but they didn't have to. The breaking-up noises of the sinking *Minatsuki* were relayed through the water to them.

Dealey wasted no time. "All ahead!" he commanded. "There are still five Nip ships up there."

The *Harder* rose to the surface for greater speed and slogged on at a full twenty knots after the fleeing convoy. Sam Dealey was again on his cramped bridge, and as he watched the white V of waves curl back from the sharp nose of the *Harder,* he thought of the other Jap ships the sub had sent to the bottom.

Sagara Maru, 7,189 tons, had been the first of them, a converted seaplane tender sunk in Japanese waters. On the second patrol, the *Harder* had gone so close to the Japanese coast that they had been able to see car lights on the coastal highway. Near Tokyo, the big American fish had gotten to work in deadly earnest. One after the other, she had sunk them: *Koyo Maru, Yolo Maru, Kachisan Maru, Kowa Maru,* and *Daishin Maru*—5,272 tons in all. The hard-hitting *Harder* had proudly returned to the subbase at Fremantle,

Australia, with a broom lashed to her periscope, symbolic of having swept the Jap seas.

"They've seen us, sir!" broke in a lookout.

A rakish Nip destroyer had heeled over in a fast turn and started for the *Harder*.

"Clear the bridge!" commanded Dealey. "Pull the plug!"

The *Harder* slid beneath the water. "Up periscope!" commanded Dealey.

But this Jap skipper was a canny one. He did not come *down the slot* like the skipper of the *Minatsuki* had done. He zigzagged his fast craft at top speed to make good tracking impossible.

"Down periscope!"

They could hear the throbbing of the fast propellers to one side of them.

"Up periscope! Down periscope! Forward room, make ready the bow tubes! Open outer doors! Up periscope! Mark!"

The hungry TDC gobbled in the data.

"Here she comes! Mark! Stand by to fire! Fire one! Fire two! Fire three! Fire four! Fire five! Fire six!"

Six deadly *tin-fish* hissed from the bow tubes. Dealey held his breath as they sped toward the racing tin can, but at the last possible second, the destroyer swerved hard to starboard, and the six-torpedo spread shot harmlessly past the bows.

"Rig for depth charges! Silent running!"

The crew knew what was coming next. They didn't have long to wait as the *Harder* headed down deep. Something clicked, seemingly right next to the pressure hull, and then the first depth charge exploded, followed quickly by four more explosions. The *Harder* shuddered as each *ash-can* let go with 230 pounds of explosives. Deeper and deeper she burrowed.

Dealey glanced at the depth gauge. The *Harder* was almost at her safe depth. More ash-cans thudded off. A report came in that some electrical controls had gone out of action. "Shift to hand controls!" came the order.

Men moved swiftly. But something was wrong. The *Harder* should have leveled off like the thoroughbred she was, but instead, she dived deeper beyond her maximum depth. A spurt of water, like a knife blade, shot through a seam opened a little by one of the explosions. The pressure hull creaked ominously.

Still, the *Harder* dived...250 feet...275 feet...three hundred feet. "*All free hands aft!*" yelled the diving officer. The men not needed to control the boat forced their way up against the increasing angle.

The diving officer clawed his way to the man who operated the stern planes. A new man, in his excitement at being depth-charged for the first time, had turned the hand control wheel the wrong way!

The diving officer reversed the wheel. Slowly, the creaking boat began to level. But her delicate balance had been disturbed, and she began to angle toward the surface as though eager to meet those deadly ash-cans erupting steadily above her. "*All hands forward!*"

Once again, the mad race uphill. Slowly, the submarine responded until she was once again under control. Taut-faced men eyed each other without speaking. It had been a close thing.

The *Harder* slowly drew away from the angry depth charges.

The new stern plane man was sent to see Commander Dealey, and he was probably more afraid of his skipper than he was of the depth charges. He explained what happened, then waited for a rawhiding, Texas style.

Commander Dealey smiled. "Son," he said, "there is room aboard a submarine for everything *but a mistake*. Dismissed!" Nothing more was said about the incident, but Sam Dealey made a mental note to write out a report of it to turn in at the subbase headquarters in Fremantle. The next time it happened, on the *Harder* or any other sub, it might end in a disaster.

"Secure from battle stations," was the command. "Third section on watch."

The *Harder* had work to do. The first mission was to pick up a team of British and Australian commandos that had been operating behind Japanese lines on Borneo for two years. Three other submarines had failed to find them.

The second mission, and actually the more important of the two, was to scout the Japanese fleet based on the old United States Navy Asiatic base at Tawi Tawi. The place would be alive with anti-submarine vessels, plane patrols, and possibly mines.

The commandos came first. The *Harder* surfaced and headed for the rendezvous.

Sam Dealey was a professional Navy officer who had graduated from the United States Naval Academy in 1930. After a tour aboard the battlewagon *Nevada*, he had been ordered to the New London Naval Submarine Base in Connecticut for submarine training. He had passed the course successfully with high grades and was ordered to duty in Hawaii aboard the older type S boats.

In 1940, Sam had been transferred to a destroyer,

the USS *Reuben James,* where he served under an old friend and Academy classmate named Tex Edwards. Before 1940 had ended, he was back on submarine duty, commanding the S-20, and he was still in command of the boat when World War Two broke out. About that time, he learned that the *Reuben James* had been torpedoed by a German U-boat off Iceland and had gone down, taking Tex Edwards with her.

Sam had immediately asked for combat duty but had been turned down. Instead, he stayed aboard the aging S-20, which was being used as a sort of guinea pig to test new methods of warfare. It wasn't until April of 1943 that Sam Dealey got his wish. He took command of the brand-new fleet-type submarine USS *Harder* at New London, Connecticut, and later on in the year pointed her nose toward the Pacific theatre of war.

* * *

It was almost noon the day after the *Harder* had sunk the *Minatsuki.* The big sub was traveling submerged when a radar contact was made.

"Destroyer, sir, from the size of the pip," reported the radarman.

"Up periscope!"

Sam Dealey began his patient stalking again. Sound picked up the noise of fast propellers. Dealey *walked* his periscope until he saw the target, a big Japanese tin can heading directly toward the invisible *Harder.*

"Down periscope!"

The sound grew louder. Crewmen wet their lips and spoke in whispers.

"Up periscope!" Dealey was silent for a time. "She's zigzagging."

Down, up, down, up, and down again slid the big periscope. Then it stayed up.

"Mark!" said the skipper.

Seconds ticked past. Then the commands came in rapid sequence. "Stand by to fire! Fire one! Fire two! Fire three!"

Fifteen seconds dragged by. Dealey grunted in timing with a distant explosion. "Right under the bridge!"

The second explosion came. "Aft! Near the stern! The third fish is a miss."

It didn't matter. Dealey stared, fascinated, as a third and far greater explosion rocked the air and sent violent percussion waves against the *Harder*. A leaping column of smoke and flames stained the sky. The destroyer's stern went down, standing the lean vessel nearly on end. Then she was gone. One minute after the first torpedo hit, the 2,100-ton *Hayanami* of the Imperial Japanese Navy no longer existed.

The *Harder* could be proud of herself. Within the space of sixteen hours, she had accounted for two enemy destroyers. Captain Tichenor looked at Sam Dealey. "In three years of warfare in the Pacific theatre, no United States submarine has ever sunk more than one enemy destroyer, Sam," he said.

Sam Dealey smiled grimly. "I haven't forgotten Tex Edwards and the *Reuben James*."

The exec turned from the scope at the same time the soundman reported, "Fast screws! Sounds like an A/S vessel!"

Somewhere up above, a fast vessel had turned on a

dime and was racing to get the *Harder*. The *Harder's* periscope disappeared, leaving behind only a tiny swirling eddy.

The roaring of the screws sounded like an express train crossing a trestle. "Rig for depth charges! Silent running!" was Dealey's command.

The words were hardly out of his mouth when the first click came, followed by a shocking explosion. Men were hurled to the steel decks of the sub, a water pipe broke, and cork insulation and flaking paint drifted down. One after the other, the ash-cans burst. Light bulbs shattered in the *Harder*.

There was always an amateur statistician in any crew. Naturally, the *Harder* had one. He cocked a knowing eye upward as a depth charge seemed to explode right next to the hull. "Number seventeen," he said cheerfully.

"Stow that!" a sweating chief petty officer yelled as he plugged a spurting leak.

But number seventeen seemed to be the last of them. After four hours, the *Harder* crept slowly to periscope depth, and the long tube slid upward with Dealey riding the training handles to where he could stand. Hardly had water cleared from the lens when he saw a sight that tripled his heartbeat and dried out his throat.

"Dive! Dive! Dive!" he roared.

The big sub went down with a rush.

Dealey turned from the periscope. "Six Nip tin cans," he said matter-of-factly.

For a tense moment, even the veterans of the *Harder* were a little worried.

Dealey thoughtfully rubbed his jaw. "Maybe we

ought to take a crack at them at that," he mused, with one eye half closed.

Complete silence from the waiting men.

Dealey yawned elaborately. "On the other hand," he said, "we still have to pick up those boys on North Borneo. *Really,* we should do *that* first."

He ordered the course set for the rendezvous.

The *Harder* was forty-eight hours late when she surfaced off the rendezvous point the night of June 8, 1944, thanks to the *Minatsuki* and the *Hayanami.* During daylight hours, the unseen eye of the periscope had seen Jap patrols slogging along the beaches.

Major Jinkins, an Australian commando on a special mission, was taken ashore in a rubber boat. Later during the night, the *Harder* moved out into deeper water with six bearded, emaciated commandos stuffing themselves on fresh bread, ice cream, steaks, and milk. Two years of hell in the steaming jungles of Borneo were behind them. But they weren't quite on the way back to Australia. Not yet. The *Harder* had another mission to perform before it was through.

By the spring of 1944, the Japanese had pretty well figured out the American grand strategy in the Pacific. They expected the hard-hitting Americans to strike the Mariana Islands. To oppose the Americans, the Japanese had formed a plan that called for strikes against the Americans by the Japanese Mobile Fleet temporarily based at Tawi Tawi. Admiral Nimitz, supreme American commander in the Pacific, had stationed submarines to keep an eye on the ships at Tawi Tawi. The *Harder* was to be one of them.

It had been left up to Commander Dealey to patrol the Sulu Archipelago to Zamboanga on the Island of

Mindanao, then to cross Basilan Strait and return to Australia. The *Harder* had plenty of fuel in her tanks and some torpedoes left. Sam Dealey's fifth war patrol wasn't over as yet.

The *Harder* was twenty miles north of Sibutu Passage and making good time on the surface. "Nip float plane at nine o'clock high!" cried a lookout.

The float plane immediately tipped over into a screaming dive. She had seen the slim silhouette splitting the calm seas. But she was a little too late. The *Harder* crash-dived and was gone. Aerial bombs crumped in the water without effect.

At sunset, the *Harder* surfaced and headed again for Tawi Tawi. "Two pips, sir!" reported radar. "Destroyers, I think!"

Down went the *Harder,* deep beneath the darkening seas, while soundman and radarman worked steadily, positioning the enemy.

Now and then, the soundman picked up an ominous noise. *Pinggg...pinggg...pinggg...* It was the noise of the Japanese echo-ranging apparatus feeling about for enemy subs.

They were about eight miles from the anchorage at Tawi Tawi when the *Harder* came up and Dealey made a periscope sweep. He whistled softly. Two destroyers were approaching the *Harder* on the beautiful moonlit sea.

"Battle stations torpedo!" came the command. The bell clanged immediately.

Then the silent, deadly stalking began again, with the periscope sliding up for a snap look, then down again. Now and then, the *ping* sound let the crew of the

Harder know that the Japanese were looking for them, too.

Dealey studied the two deadly, slim shapes. At three thousand yards, both vessels turned thirty degrees to starboard. It was just what Dealey wanted. Orders were rapped out. The outer doors of the torpedo tubes grinned open in anticipation.

The bow of one of the destroyers showed just beyond the bow of the closer of the speeding pair. "Mark!" snapped Dealey. "Stand by to fire! Steady...fire one! Fire two! Fire three! Fire four!"

Hard palms pressed down on firing buttons.

Dealey wet his lips as he studied the torpedo tracks. Number one shot past the bow of the closer destroyer. Then number two struck hard and true into the bow of the nearer one, and the third torpedo lanced through thin metal plating just below the bridge with a thunderous explosion. The last of the four seemed to pass harmlessly astern.

"Hard right rudder! All ahead full!" The *Harder* swung away to avoid hitting the doomed destroyer. There was no time to watch her death throes. There was another tin can still afloat.

Thirty seconds ticked by as the *Harder* maneuvered for another attack on the second destroyer. Then there was a tremendous explosion which shook the sub as a terrier shakes a rat. Dealey saw the first destroyer literally rip apart. "Boilers let go!" he yelled.

There was another loud explosion, not quite as close as the first. Dealey stared unbelievingly. Silhouetted against a glare of flame, he saw the second A/S vessel explode.

He grinned. "That last torpedo wasn't wasted! She

hit the second Nip! His ammunition magazines just let go!"

Men were slammed violently to the steel decks of the sub from the shaking up she was getting, but they were grinning, too. "A doubleheader!" yelled one of them.

The exec threw his hat on the deck. "Hit 'em again, *Harder!*" he cried.

"Score three and four this patrol," said Captain Tichenor.

Dealey waited ten minutes and then surfaced. There was nothing to fear now. Steam and smoke hung over the water like a shroud where the first tin can had destroyed herself with her exploding boilers. There was nothing where the second A/S had gone down but a lighted buoy floating on the oily waters.

One after the other, the Americans came up on deck to view the place where two fighting vessels had gone down in seconds. It was eerie up there on the top of the deadly *Harder,* with the water swashing up and down against her sleek sides. Eerie and quiet, quiet as the grave after the hell of the destruction some minutes before. None of those men would forget that moment as long as they lived.

Later reports proved that the first destroyer had been the nineteen-hundred-ton *Tanikaze,* while the second one was never identified and may have been an older destroyer on A/S patrol. Identified or not, it was certain that the *Harder* had sunk her.

* * *

The *Harder* moved away at top speed. It was midnight, 24:00 hours naval time, when they heard a roaring noise rapidly approaching. Before they could crash-dive, a Japanese float plane shot out of the darkness and practically dragged its float across the deck. Bombs shook the *Harder* as she dived, but no damage was done. In a little while, she surfaced and kept up her patrol.

When morning came, the *Harder* was a few miles from Tawi Tawi. Two destroyers were sighted a long way off. Patrol planes droned lazily across the clear sky. It was a busy place and downright unhealthy for a lone American sub that was only interested in sinking the whole Japanese Mobile Fleet before it returned to Fremantle.

Late in the afternoon, the radarman made a fat contact. "Big stuff!" he said excitedly. "Man! Look at those fat pips!"

Sam Dealey couldn't resist a look-see. He saw three battleships, a quartet of cruisers, and six to eight tin cans, all moving fast under a protective umbrella of planes. The two biggest battlewagons were sure to be the giants *Yamato* and *Musashi*.

The periscope moved slowly back and forth like the head of a sea monster looking for prey. The task force covered at least twenty square miles of water. The big battlewagons were in the center of a box of cruisers, while a semicircle of destroyers led the way, with other destroyers on either flank and the planes circling high overhead.

Dealey spoke as he studied the big battlewagons. "Those are the *mystery* ships alright—*Yamato* and *Musashi*."

"Sixty-three thousand tons," said Tichenor, "or half

again the weight displacement of *our* biggest battle-ships. Main batteries of nine eighteen-inch guns, largest of any navy in the world."

"Why did they build them?" asked the exec.

"World conquest," said Tichenor dryly.

Dealey stiffened. Black smoke had erupted near one of the big battlewagons. The sound of three distant explosions carried to the *Harder*. There was no time to figure out what had happened. A Jap destroyer had swung out of line and was splitting the blue water toward the *Harder*. Probably the sub had been seen by a plane.

"Dive! Dive! Dive!" commanded Dealey.

The *Harder* slipped through the water, then eased up again to periscope depth. Dealey whistled thinly between his teeth. "Bows on! She's really making knots! Smoke screen between us and the task force."

Dealey watched the wedge shape of the oncoming bows. The only chance was for a *down-the-throat* shot aimed squarely at the nose of the target and calculated to hit her if she veered either way. But if you should miss at such close range...

The destroyer's bow wave diminished. The Japanese skipper was smart. He was going to make a thorough search.

Pinggg...pinggg...pinggg... Echo-ranging was at work.

Now it was cat-and-mouse as the two deadly vessels felt about for each other like blind wrestlers waiting for a chance. Depth charges against torpedoes. Speed against skill.

"Fast screws!" reported sound suddenly. "Starboard beam!"

There was no time to think about the second A/S. The first destroyer was echo-ranging steadily on the *Harder*. The bow angle was zero, still coming head-on, and the Japanese were feeling about with sound antennae. Sam sneaked another look. The bow wave was curling higher and faster. The periscope had been spotted!

"Make ready the bow tubes! Open outer doors! Stand by! Steady... Fire one! Fire two! Fire three!"

Three tin-fish hissed from the tubes. Range fifteen hundred yards, gyro angles near zero—a real *down-the-throat* shot.

"Fast screws closing in, starboard beam!" reported sound.

No time to look! "All ahead, full, right full rudder. *Take 'er deep!*" snapped Sam Dealey.

The depth gauge marked eighty feet, and it was fifty-five seconds after the first torpedo shot when the first blast came, followed five seconds later by a second blast. The *Harder* was passing almost underneath the doomed A/S when the explosions began, and it was far worse than a depth charging. The *Harder* shook and shivered. She pitched and rolled, scattering men about like dice in a cup. Bulbs shattered and cork insulation floated down in a cloud. A deafening series of rumblings penetrated the diving sub.

Sam Dealey clung to a support with one hand. "Sounds like her magazines or boilers, or both, have let go." He grinned wanly. "Good thing for the old *Harder* that ship explosions vent upward instead of downward, or we'd be headed for Davy Jones's locker."

Depth charges on the deck of the sinking vessel began to explode. A barometer flew from its fitting on a bulkhead. A chain lashed out from its hook like a striking rattler and knocked a young crewman cold.

One of the British agents was wan and drawn with jungle fever, and the sweat of heat and fear ran down his bearded face. He eyed Sam Dealey. "I say, old thing, would you mind taking us *back* to Borneo?" he asked dryly.

The hunt went on for hours. Depth charges and aerial bombs felt about for the sub. *Pinging* went on and on and then finally died away altogether. When the *Harder* surfaced at last, there was no sign of the target. Nothing but the dim yellow pinpoint of a lighted buoy bobbing about three miles astern of the sub.

The *Harder* stayed around for three more days in those deadly waters. On June 10, 1944, she reported that the Mobile Fleet had left the Tawi Tawi anchorage. There was a good reason for them doing so, but Sam Dealey and the crew of the *Harder* didn't know it at the time. Admiral Soemu Toyoda, commander-in-chief of the Japanese Combined Fleet, could not believe that one submarine had done all that damage in the Sibutu Passage. He believed that Tawi Tawi was the goal of a massive concentration of American submarines. He reported to his superiors that he did not now have enough destroyers to protect his capital ships. He decided to leave.

The Combined Japanese Fleet, the ships from Tawi Tawi and a carrier striking force, blundered about together and ran head-on into the American Striking Force. The result was the smashing defeat of the Japanese in the Battle of the Philippine Sea, which forever destroyed the Japanese Imperial Navy as an effective striking weapon. It was a battle that took place because the *Harder,* with a top crew and a hard-fighting commander, had accounted for five destroyers in as many days.

Actually, with the exception of the *Redfin,* another American sub, there were no other American submarines near Tawi Tawi at the time the *Harder* was having her field day.

Officially, the *Harder* was credited with sinking three Japanese destroyers on that famous fifth war patrol and damaging at least two more, although some sources state she actually sank five. In any case, her patrol had far-reaching effects in destroying Japanese war plans and aiding in the destruction of her fleet in the Philippine Sea.

The *Harder* was met at Fremantle by General Douglas MacArthur, who presented Commander Sam Dealey with the Army Distinguished Service Cross. The other officers and the crew were also recognized with various decorations, while the gallant *Harder* received the Presidential Unit Citation for herself and her crew.

Commander Samuel Davis Dealey, Jr. was awarded the Medal of Honor, but he took the *Harder* out on her sixth war patrol before the decoration was presented to him. The gallant *Harder* and her crew did not return from that patrol. The submarine was destroyed by an A/S vessel with all hands on August 24, 1944, somewhere off the coast of Luzon in the Philippines.

Three days before that fateful day, a five-boat wolf pack of submarines, led by Commander Sam Dealey, had engaged two enemy convoys, sinking ten ships and driving the remainder back into the harbor. The

Matsuwa and the *Hiburi,* frigates, were the last of sixteen vessels in all sunk by Sam Dealey and his crew.

Camp Dealey on Guam was named after Sam Dealey, and today, there is a building called Dealey Center at the United States New London Submarine Base. The battle cry of his submarine is still well remembered in the Submarine Force.

"Hit 'em again, *Harder!*"

EIGHT
SOME KIND OF MIRACLE
LLOYD L. BURKE

THE CARRYING PARTY from Company G of the Fifth Cavalry Regiment, First Cavalry Division, slogged along across the wide valley at the base of rugged Hill Two Hundred. The *chogi* party was heavily laden with ammunition, explosive satchel charges, and other lethal odds and ends so necessary in the art of modern warfare.

Now and then, the tired men looked at the looming hill. They had looked up at a lot of hills in Korea, and they hadn't seen one they liked yet. The reason was simple enough. Korean or Chinese Reds usually held those hills, and they had to be taken one by one. Hill Two Hundred was a key spot, with its heights overlooking a view of the Imjin River and quite a parcel of other terrain. The division needed that hill, but as usual, the Chinese Reds held it.

The *chogi* party was led by the company executive officer, who looked out of place beside the big, carrying men of the party. Lloyd L. Burke, First Lieutenant in the Regular Army, was short, of slight build, and wore glasses. But the eyes behind those shining glasses were intent on Hill Two Hundred. The Second Battalion of the Fifth Cavalry was up there, at least a good part of the way up there, hanging on by fingers and toes, or so it seemed, to a ridge thirty feet wide, about two hundred feet below the crest of the hill. That was as far as they had managed to get, and there they stayed.

The *chogi* party started up the slope. Now and then, they heard the stuttering of a machine gun and the more rapid firing of a Red burp gun. Sparklets of fire danced for a time along the ridge, and then it was quiet again. A fifty-seven-millimeter recoilless rifle cracked, and the echo slammed back and forth between the valley walls.

"Cavalry," jeered a tired carrier. He shook his head. "This outfit ever really have hosses, sir?"

Burke turned with a quick smile. "Yes," he said in a soft Arkansas drawl. "Back in the years before World War Two."

"They ever *use* 'em, Lootenant?"

Burke nodded. "Plenty, in the old days. Civil War, Indian Wars, and a few other hot places. The old Fifth Cavalry made a famous charge at Gaines Mill in 1862 during the Civil War."

The carrier grinned. "They do any good?"

Burke's eyes were on the hill. The sound of erratic firing drifted down to the carrying party. It seemed to Lloyd Burke that the firing had a tired sound, almost a losing sound. The First Cavalry Division wasn't accustomed to losing a fight.

"Sir?" persisted the curious carrier.

Burke turned a little. "Fifty-five casualties," he said quietly.

Another man laughed. "Hardly a spit in the bucket!"

Burke was looking up at that ominous hill again. "They started out with five hundred men," he said.

The carriers glanced at each other. They knew that the First Cavalry Division had fought with distinction throughout the Pacific theatre in World War Two. They had been proud of the big yellow shoulder patch they wore, with the black slanted bar and horse's head, but that had been because of the division's record as dismounted fighting men during World War Two. Even now, fighting in Korea, few of them had ever heard much about the proud record of the old Fifth United States Cavalry.

"Take a break," said Burke, as he stopped near an outpost. He stayed on his feet, looking up at that hill. Company G, his old company, was at the very tip of the battalion position. There couldn't be many of them left by now.

Almost as though he read the officer's mind, one of the men spoke quietly. "Old *George* must be catching it up there."

"Yeah, *if they's any of them left*," said another soldier. He looked at Burke.

They all knew what he was thinking. Lloyd Burke was the regiment's *old man* from length of service in Korea. He rarely spoke about himself, but the whole Fifth Regiment knew him. He was a fighting man, with thirteen months of combat behind him. He had a Distinguished Service Cross earned in November of 1950 for blowing a way through a Commie roadblock near Samso-Ri, and a Silver Star earned in the months after the fight at Samso-Ri. He had been awarded a

Bronze Star for the destruction of a machine-gun nest, and he held two Purple Hearts as well.

"Lookit him," said a lolling private out of the side of his mouth. He jerked his head toward the short figure of Burke. "He's itchin' all over to get into this fight too."

A corporal spat. "If I was him, with his time in this man's war, I'd be back in a bunker fifty miles from here, with track shoes on, waiting for the word to head back to Japan."

The rattling of rifle and machine-gun fire came down to them as the wind shifted. An officer came from the outpost and spoke to Burke. "Beats me why you don't stay out of the shooting gallery when you have a chance, Scooter," he said wearily, using Burke's nickname.

The light flashed from Burke's glasses as he looked at the officer. "What's the pitch up there?"

The officer shrugged. "Fox Company, under-strength, tried to take the hilltop. Got ten yards. Easy Company tried it. They're pinned down."

"Who's next?"

The officer studied Burke. "George Company, Scooter."

Burke rubbed his jaw. "Who's taking them in?"

"Sergeant Foster, senior NCO George Company hasn't an officer left to lead them."

"That's where you're wrong. I'll take them in. Foster is a good man, but that's *my* company up there."

"Use your head, Scooter! Go back while you have a chance. This is none of your affair."

The little officer turned to a non-com with the carrying party. "You know where to take this stuff. Take over. See you."

The men watched Burke climb the hill. "I knew they'd never keep him outta that fight," said one of them, shaking his head.

* * *

It was the twenty-fifth day of Operation Commando, and the Second Battalion of the Fifth Cavalry had been held up for several days at Hill Two Hundred, under-strength and short of officers. The officer scrambling up that rugged and deadly hill meant to do something about it. He usually did something about such problems.

Lloyd L. Burke was a Stuttgart, Arkansas, boy who had wanted to be a star athlete at Stuttgart High. He dreamed of having a big S on his school sweater. But Lloyd never quite made it. He had the spirit all right, but not the size or strength. He ended up in the band where he was good enough to win the State Drum Solo Championship. He had graduated and entered Henderson State College but had left school in his first year to enlist in the Army for World War Two, where he had served in Italy with the combat engineers.

In the year after the war, he had re-entered Henderson State College. One day, he had seen a notice that the school's most distinguished graduate of the Reserve Officers Training Corps would be entitled to apply for a Regular Army commission. This was just what he had been looking for. In 1949, he received the commission and entered the rough and tough Infantry School at Fort Benning, Georgia.

By October of 1950, he was busy at his chosen profession in Korea, fighting a war. He was awarded the

Distinguished Service Cross and the Silver Star, the latter for a daring raid in August of 1951. He already had two Purple Hearts for being wounded in November 1950 and in January 1951.

Scooter Burke approached George Company, or what was left of it. Thirty-five tired men eyed their old executive officer. They knew they had to make the attack. There was no looking back for help. It was up to them.

Sergeant Foster smiled wearily. "I thought you'd be in the States by now, sir."

Burke shook his head. "Brief me," he said shortly.

Foster showed the officer what was expected of the company. Burke got hold of a fifty-seven-millimeter recoilless rifle and had it moved as far forward in the trench as he could. He sighted it on the nearest enemy bunker, or strong point, and fired point-blank into it with about as much effect as if he were throwing spitballs.

Sergeant Foster shrugged. "You see what I mean, sir?"

Burke nodded. He drew out his forty-five-caliber automatic pistol and led some of the men forward to test the enemy resistance. He tested it all right. Chinese grenades flew through the air and crashed all about them.

Burke crouched in the trench and looked about at the tired men. They were expecting him to perform some kind of miracle. He took a Garand M1 rifle and again went as far forward in the trench as he could, rested the heavy rifle in a rough embrasure, and waited. He could see the Commie grenadier rise a little, hurl his grenade, and disappear.

"Just like a target in a shooting gallery," said Foster.

The officer sighted at the exact place where he had last seen the grenadier. Up came the grenadier for a split second, and the Garand cracked flatly. Down went the grenadier. Burke waited. Then a grenade sailed through the air and coughed, scattering fragments that clattered murderously on the rocks. Scooter had seen the arm come up and the head. He fired, but a moment later, the grenadier was in business again.

Some of the men shook their heads as the officer emptied the clip and then reloaded. It was a cinch he was off shooting form that day.

Burke leaned the Garand against the side of the trench. Before Foster could stop him, he had leaped from the trench, rolled to his feet, and sprinted for the enemy trench twenty-five yards away. He struck the dirt close to a rock wall and flattened himself. Out of the corner of his eye, he saw the grenades sailing overhead to crash in or near G Company's trench.

His breath was harsh in his throat as he lay there. Then he saw a grenade drop straight toward him, and he could hear the trench defenders jabbering at each other. He caught the deadly egg in mid-air, drew back his arm, and pitched it back into the trench. It blew almost at once, but there was another one in the air. Once again, Burke fielded it and pitched it back with all his strength. Another grenade came flying to replace the second one, and he caught it, too.

"Three strikes! You're out!" he grunted as he drew his pistol and slipped off the safety. He knew well enough he couldn't take much more of that deadly ball game.

He stood up, placed his free hand on the lip of the trench, and vaulted easily into it.

Two staring Reds faced him as he crouched, pulled the trigger, and felt the big automatic buck back in his hand. The first Red went down, and the second had no time to fire before a heavy forty-five slug dropped him across his dead partner.

Burke wiped his face. Despite his danger, he felt better. His Garand shooting hadn't been off after all. Five Chinese lay dead where he had been shooting at what he had thought was but one grenadier. Beyond them was a crumpled group of five more dead Chinese killed by the grenades he had hurled back at them.

He crept along the trench with ready automatic until he found a communications trench leading to the next strong point of the Reds. He picked up enemy grenades and hurled them into the second line. There were shrill screams and yells. When the smoke cleared, he saw that the next line of bunkers was empty of Chinese. They had pulled back to yet another defense line.

He wet his lips as he watched Chinese grenades flying to his left and American grenades passing them to his right. The air was thick with the smoke of explosions, and the continual crumping of the grenades was rough on the ears. It was no place for a peaceful man. He spotted a Korean grave and began to work his way around its rim, tensing himself for a dash to his lines.

Then his jaw dropped as he looked down into an enemy trench winding its way around the rear of Hill Two Hundred. It was crammed with Commies, and many of them were dropping shells into the tubes of their mortars, laughing and chattering as the mortar-propelling charges coughed and sent the projectiles wobbling through the smoky air. The Second Battalion of the Fifth would be cut to pieces with such a concentration of mortars.

Scooter didn't waste any time. The god of battles had given him a break and he recognized it. It was up to a good soldier to take advantage of it. He panted back to George Company and dragged Foster to him. "Give me a machine gun, Foster," he snapped.

The sergeant waved a hand at a light machine gun. "That's the only one we have in working order, sir."

"I'll take it then!"

The sergeant looked at the sweating officer. "What do *we* do, sir?"

"Come a-runnin' when I need you!"

The little officer, who had been too small to make the basketball team and the football team back at Stuttgart High, now took the light machine gun and three cans of ammunition and climbed out of the trench, lugging the heavy weight across the broken ground while mortar projectiles sailed over his head.

He made the burial mound without being seen and quickly set up the machine gun. He threaded in the first belt and crouched behind the deadly weapon, studying the trench filled with laughing, chattering Chinese. "Sure are a mess of them," he said to himself as he made his sight adjustments and loosened the traverse screw. If those Reds sent in a mass attack, there would be nothing left of the battered Second Battalion.

Scooter drew in a deep breath and let out half of it. He loaded the chamber, then touched off the gun.

The first mortar crew never knew what hit them as the slugs chewed them down. The surviving enemy troops panicked, and many of them threw away their weapons to dive over the back of the trench and stream down the reverse slope with hot slugs whipping into them and past them.

The machine gun jammed. Burke worked swiftly to clear it. He looked up in time to see a Red hurling grenades at him. The Red was off form that day, but amid the confusion of smoke, whining metal fragments, and flying dirt, Scooter felt something slash across his left hand. The Red went down as Foster led up his handful of George Company men. Garand rifles began to crack in unison with the machine gun.

Blood dripped from Lloyd Burke's left hand as he fired steadily. The machine gun was almost too hot to touch. Sergeant Foster dropped beside the officer. "Look at them run!" he yelled above the crackling of the machine gun.

The Chinese outnumbered G Company ten to one, but they were convinced that G Company had launched a mass attack. That devil-gun beside the Korean grave never seemed to stop whipping them with hot metal.

Scooter ripped off his bloodstained field jacket and wrapped it around the hot barrel of the gun. He picked it from the tripod and jerked his head at Sergeant Foster. Together, the two fighting men advanced on the running, screaming Chinese, spraying them with machine-gun and rifle fire until the machine-gun ran dry. Burke dropped the useless gun and yelled.

"Grenades! Grenades! Grenades!"

The men of George Company pitched grenades to Scooter Burke. The little officer darted toward the opening into a bunker, pulled the pins on two grenades, and pitched them in, diving to one side a second or so before they erupted. A blast of smoke and gas surged out into the trench. Scooter wiped the sweat from his face and then stared at five Chinese who, their hands in the air, unmarked by wounds, stumbled through the smoke.

"Let's go, George Company!" yelled Scooter as he led the cheering troopers in a hell-for-leather charge down Hill Two Hundred, reminiscent of the old horse-mounted days of the Fifth United States Cavalry at Gaines Mill in 1862. When the smoke of battle cleared, they held the hill, having suffered two casualties, while more than two hundred Chinese lay dead.

The curious troopers found that the Chinese had burrowed deep into Hill Two Hundred and had crammed it with supplies for a long stay. They hadn't figured on Scooter Burke.

Men of G Company authenticated the fact that Lieutenant Burke had personally put three machine-gun nests and two mortar emplacements out of action and had accounted for more than one hundred of the enemy on that bloody hill overlooking the Imjin. Men of the Fifth Cavalry never think of it as Hill Two Hundred but rather as Scooter Burke's Peak.

The motto of the Fifth United States Cavalry is *Loyalty and Courage*. First Lieutenant Lloyd L. Burke followed that motto in the Korean Conflict of 1950-1953. For his exploits on Hill Two Hundred, October 28, 1951, he was decorated with the Medal of Honor. No fighting man deserved it more.

A LOOK AT: THE COMPLETE SOUTHWESTERN SERIES

FOUR FULL LENGTH WESTERN NOVELS

Take a journey with frontiersman, Quint Kershaw—a man as strong as the land he tamed —in this four-book western collection by Gordon D. Shirreffs.

In *The Untamed Breed,* Quint Kershaw is a man yearning to master the wild West, while three women long to conquer this trapper's heart—a Shoshoni maiden, an Easterner who tries to tame him, and the Mexican heiress whose love comes with a price.

Responding to his government's orders to assist the invasion of New Mexico, estate owner and frontiersman Kershaw finds his greatest challenge in his wife Lupita and her fierce loyalty to her Spanish ancestry in *Bold Legend.*

In *Glorieta Pass*, Kershaw is called upon by Kit Carson to fight for the Union—his mission is to help preserve New Mexico from a Confederate onslaught. His whole family is caught up in the conflict and Quint himself comes face-to-face with an old flame—now suddenly available and as ravishing as ever.

In *The Ghost Dancers*, a band of Mexican outlaws who hunted scalps for bounty were unaware that their deadly spree had earned them a powerful enemy. Major Alec Kershaw and his two allies, Chief Baishan and Anne Sinclair, weren't about to see the Apache annihilated. In the final showdown, Alec had nothing but a steady hand and the determination to protect those—and the land—he loved.

AVAILABLE NOW

ABOUT THE AUTHOR

Gordon D. Shirreffs published more than 80 western novels, 20 of them juvenile books, and John Wayne bought his book title, Rio Bravo, during the 1950s for a motion picture, which Shirreffs said constituted *"the most money I ever earned for two words."* Four of his novels were adapted to motion pictures, and he wrote a Playhouse 90 and the Boots and Saddles TV series pilot in 1957.

A former pulp magazine writer, he survived the transition to western novels without undue trauma, earning the admiration of his peers along the way. The novelist saw life a bit cynically from the edge of his funny bone and described himself as looking like a slightly parboiled owl. Despite his multifarious quips, he was dead serious about the writing profession.

Gordon D. Shirreffs was the 1995 recipient of the Owen Wister Award, given by the Western Writers of America for "a living individual who has made an outstanding contribution to the American West."

He passed in 1996.